TARGETED VOCABULARY STRATEGIES

FOR SECONDARY SOCIAL STUDIES

TINA HEAFNER & DIXIE MASSEY

Project Coordinator: Dr. Aaron Willis
Editor: Roberta Dempsey
Editorial Assistant: Lindsey Drager
Cover Illustration and Layout Design: A.R. Harter

10200 Jefferson Boulevard, P.O. Box 802
Culver City, CA 90232-0802
United States of America

(310) 839-2436
(800) 421-4246

Fax: (800) 944-5432
Fax: (310) 839-2249

www.socialstudies.com
access@socialstudies.com

ISBN 978-1-56004-688-2
Product Code: Z102

PREFACE

Twenty years ago I (Tina) began my journey as a high school social studies teacher. While my path led me to pursue university teaching after seven years in the classroom, I am still entrenched in the belief that my preparation of teachers has to be grounded in the realities of American public schools. As a result, I have spent much of my time in higher education observing how teachers teach and exploring how students learn in secondary social studies classrooms. Over the past eight years I have taught a social studies methods course at a local high school and facilitated an afterschool tutoring program to help struggling secondary students learn social studies. The lessons that I gleaned from these experiences are the impetus for writing this book.

Originally, I thought the source of student frustration and lack of academic achievement was related to missing reading comprehension skills; however, over time I came to understand that most high school students are in general good readers and exercise sound literacy skills. The students that I worked with in tutoring could read a social studies text aloud well, but struggled to put into their own words the meaning and significance of the narrative. As I guided tutors and their students each week, a reoccurring emphasis on vocabulary instruction resonated. Despite curriculum changes, grade level differences, and student literacy skill-sets, the main function of each tutoring lesson served to teach and reinforce social studies word learning. While the format of lessons might vary from review of word lists, geographical mapping of terms, to textbook reading, the main source of student struggles was the gap in familiarity with social studies terms and concepts. Overwhelmingly, student comprehension and content understanding was tied to social studies word awareness.

In my constant professional challenge of honing my knowledge and skills so that I might better direct the work of teachers, tutors, and students in more targeted work, I immersed myself in examining current vocabulary research. I also sought the expertise of a dear friend and literacy expert, Dr. Dixie Massey. Together we ploughed through a wealth of information to find that, while there were tons of strategies available, an organizational structure for purposefully integrating these methods into the curriculum was missing. Vocabulary teaching as we observed through our tutoring projects had to be consistent, frequent, and easily replicable. Additionally, we noted that there were specific points in the learning process in which certain strategies were more meaningful and effective. The vocabulary strategies that students used to be familiar with words were not the same methods they used to connect words to broader concepts. While students were learning words with isolated strategies, they were not able to translate vocabulary learning into consistent improvement in academic achievement. They could recognize words, define words but could not use words to promote comprehension while reading or in other contexts.

In our ongoing collaboration to understand what might be creating this learning-achievement gap, one thing stood out to both of us. Although students were systematically learning words, they were not getting repeated and authentic exposures to words throughout a unit of study. As we shifted our preparation of tutors we noted a significant change in how our students began to teach vocabulary skills and in student success. Emphasizing the significance of interconnected and relational word learning strategies, we developed a targeted process that provides the means for multiple exposures to words and word meanings. Unlike the other vocabulary frameworks, our approach provides teachers with a guide for exposing students to the same set of words in new and meaningful ways over the course of a unit.

Furthermore, implementation of other projects such as Literacy for Democracy, and interaction with content area literacy specialists have led us to recognize that contextually-based word learning is not consistent for all subject areas. Students encounter new words in different text genres than those used in other subjects. For example, when a student reads a primary source in a social studies class, unfamiliar words can not only be interpreted through contemporary definitions, but they also have meanings that may have changed over time. These words may also be no longer in use in everyday language. Of even greater significance is the role perspective writing plays in learning word meanings within a historical context. As Dixie and I concluded eight years ago in an article we co-authored, social studies teachers are literacy teachers. They teach content literacy skills that students need to be successful both in academic environments and in their broader role as citizens in a complex and ever-changing society.

Recognizing that teachers exercise the amazing craft of taking a complex process and breaking it into understandable increments, we sought to develop a social studies vocabulary book that would guide teachers and students in a purposeful approach to unraveling word learning. We hope to equip teachers and students with a vocabulary tool kit that maximizes student academic achievement. We chose to target high school social studies learners so that we could provide replicable content specific applications and examples of multiple word exposures. This book presents five instructional routines for teachers to use at key intervention points within a unit of study. Each instructional routine is aligned with recommended vocabulary strategies that effectively achieve identified word learning outcomes. Implemented together, the five instructional routines help teachers provide students with the multiple exposures necessary for true conceptual understanding. To demonstrate how these interventions work, we offer specific social studies examples that target vocabulary development.

There have been many individuals who have been instrumental in bringing this project to fruition. First and foremost, we would like to recognize the importance of the support of our families. The long hours that we devoted have been family sacrifices, too. Thanks to Victor, Victoria, and Caleb as well as John, John Patrick, and Laney for your understanding. I would also like to thank the contributions of Michelle Plaisance, an urban education doctoral candidate who provided extensive collections of research in the early stages of this project. We appreciate the support of the editorial staff at Social Studies School Service for their helpful feedback that shaped this project into our vision for a practical and meaningful teacher resource. Finally, we are grateful to our institutions who provided nurturing environments for exploration of new research and writing opportunities.

TABLE OF CONTENTS

◎ **Preface** iii

◎ **Introduction** 1

What Do We Know About Vocabulary Learning? 1

The Academic Task 4

Targeted Vocabulary Instruction 7

Using This Guide 8

◎ **Instructional Routine 1:**
Grouping and Organizing 11

Application 1: Identify Word Part Patterns 12

    Words Are All Greek to Me 12

    Grouping and Organizing Suffix Word Patterns 16

Application 2: Sort Word Lists...19

    Categories and Labels 19

    Word List, Group, Label, Add, Sequence, Outline, Title 21

Application 3: Connect Words to Concepts 23

    Concept Trees 23

    Concept Trees (Reproducible) 26

    Middle Concept..27

    Middle Concept (Reproducible) 30

Application 4: Relate Word Groups and Organization to Reading 31

   Degrees of Knowledge 31

   How Well Do I Know These Words? 32

   Predict the Pattern 33

   Predict the Pattern (Reproducible) 35

   Sort and Verify 38

   Sort and Verify (Reproducible) 40

   Sort and Verify Words in Context (Reproducible) 42

Instructional Routine 1: Summary 43

◎ Instructional Routine 2:
Mapping and Visualizing 45

Application 1: Word Organizers and Relational Mapping 46

   Word Organizers 46

   I-Chart (Reproducible) 48

   Relational Organizers 50

Application 2: Visualization Strategies 58

   Word Walls and Word Maps 58

   Word Wall (Reproducible) 60

   ABC Graffiti (Reproducible) 62

   Illustrating Meanings 66

   Word Art 72

   Visual Inventory 74

Instructional Routine 2: Summary 80

◎ Instructional Routine 3:
Comparing and Contrasting

Application 1: Compare and Contrast Organizers 82

    Venn Diagrams 82

    T-charts 83

Application 2: Continuum of Meaning 84

Application 3: Relational Analysis 86

Application 4: What Is It? What Is It Not? 88

Instructional Routine 3: Summary 93

◎ Instructional Routine 4:
Defining and Associating

Application 1: Vocabulary Manipulative Cards (VMCs) 96

Application 2: Tiered Word Sorts 99

Application 3: Sorting Degrees of Knowledge 101

    How Well Do I Know the Meaning of Words? (Reproducible) 102

Application 4: Forced Associations 103

Application 5: Squared Up 105

Application 6: Personal Vocabulary Journals (PVJs) 111

Application 7: Word of the Day 114

Application 8: Contextual Clues 116

Application 9: Roll the Die 119

Application 10: Concept Associations 125

Application 11: Memory Aids and Mnemonics 129

Instructional Routine 4: Conclusion 133

◎ **Instructional Routine 5:**
Reviewing and Playing with Words............... 135

Application 1: I Have, Who Has? 136

Application 2: Pictionary® 139

Application 3: Scattergories® 140

Application 4: Vocabulary Bingo 141

Application 5: Who Am I? 141

Application 6: Who, What, Where Am I? 144

Application 7: Vocabulary Jigsaw 146

Application 8: Taboo® 149

Instructional Routine 5: Conclusion 149

◎ **Sample Unit: World Religions**..................... 151

◎ **Resources** 159

◎ **Web sites**................................. 165

INTRODUCTION

◎ What Do We Know About Vocabulary Learning?

Academic vocabulary, the language of social studies, is essential to discipline-specific learning. For secondary students to comprehend and explore the rich narrative of social studies, they need a vocabulary tool kit that will enable them to develop the skills to understand the words they encounter as they navigate various sources of information. Academic vocabulary opens doors for students to become social studies insiders (Moore, Readence, & Rickelman, 1989) by providing the academic knowledge and skill-set necessary to effectively communicate individual perspectives drawn from multigenre and diverse texts. Learners are able to successfully contribute to a social studies dialogue in meaningful and purposeful ways using the language of the discipline. Moreover, those who have ownership of academic vocabulary possess the cultural capital and literacy skills necessary for success in a globally dynamic and interdependent society. These learners become "powerful" thinkers (NCSS Position Statement, 2009) and embody the social studies goals set forth for competent citizens and effective decision-makers. Moreover, academic knowledge is essential in developing the Common Core State Standards and national policy objectives of *NCLB*. In sum, the importance of vocabulary in social studies goes uncontested as a way to improve student academic and educational success.

Drawing upon literacy and social studies research, we present four statements that articulate what we know about vocabulary learning and its connection to content understanding. These four research-based points support our view that vocabulary learning is central to all learning, especially in social studies. We know that:

1. There is a strong relationship between vocabulary, knowledge, comprehension, and achievement.

2. The bigger the vocabulary, the greater the comprehension.

3. Vocabulary knowledge is cumulative and generative.

4. Students need frequent and authentic interactions with words.

1. There is a strong relationship between vocabulary, knowledge, comprehension, and achievement.

Student knowledge of words impacts academic achievement and directly relates to content comprehension (Baumann, Kame'enui, & Ash, 2003; Graves, 2009; Lehr, Osborn, & Hievert, 2004; Stanovich, 1986, 1993). Leading researchers (Allen, 2007; Allen & Landaker, 2005; Marzano, 2004; Stahl & Nagy, 2006) maintain that there is a strong relationship between vocabulary knowledge, academic content background knowledge, and comprehension (Anderson & Freebody, 1981; Beck & McKeown, 1991; Beck, Perfetti, & McKeown, 1982; Davis, 1994; McKeown, Beck, Omanson, & Pople, 1985). This interconnected process of learning makes vocabulary essential to improving student academic achievement.

Strong Relationship Between

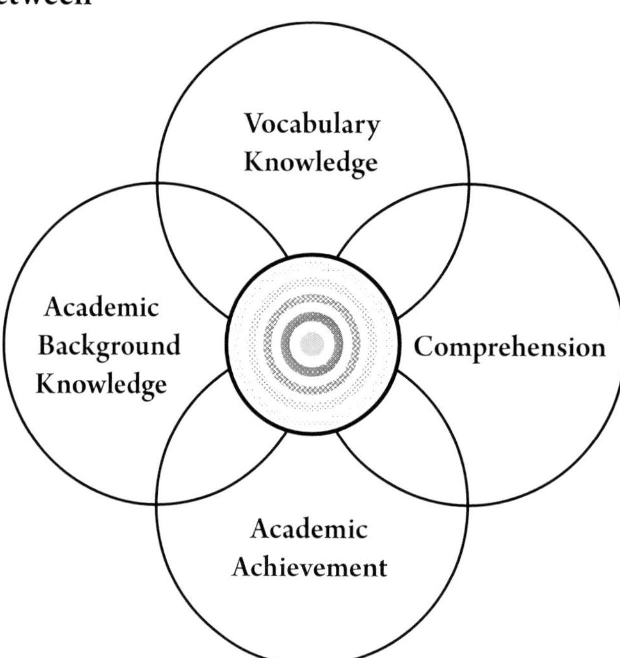

2. The bigger the vocabulary, the greater the comprehension.

The more words students know in a content area, the more able they will be to comprehend subject-specific texts they encounter in high school classes. As Stahl and Nagy (2006) summarized, "having a big vocabulary" makes students better readers (p. 9). Given the amount of reading secondary students are assigned in social studies classes, vocabulary knowledge becomes an important indicator of student success.

3. Vocabulary knowledge is cumulative and generative.

Additionally, vocabulary knowledge is cumulative and interventions over time lead to long-term gains. Yet, realized gains are not equitable for all students. Stahl and Nagy (2006) further documented that a student who has a large vocabulary learns new words more easily than a student with a smaller vocabulary. This trend of "the more words a student knows, the broader the vocabulary a student will acquire" widens over a student's school career, making dense texts such as those found in social studies difficult to access and understand for many secondary students. In this sense, vocabulary becomes the information base from which students will make inferences

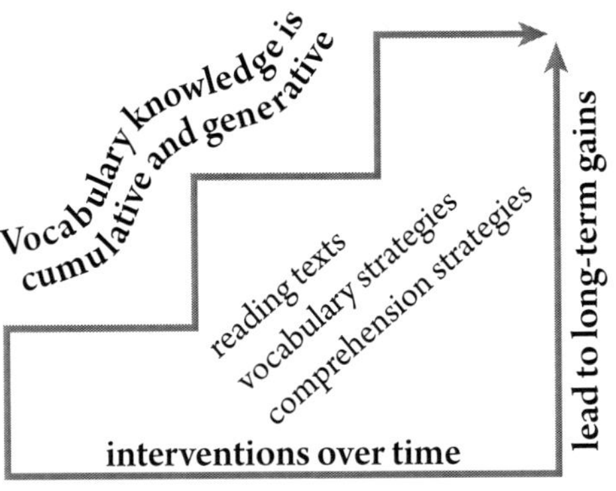

by connecting to prior knowledge, whereby cumulative content learning outcomes are realized. Further, vocabulary knowledge is generative. For example, students who recognize Greek and Latin roots are able to understand new words based on recognition of word parts. Generative word learning expands students' ability to recognize new words and to decipher word meanings from existing schema.

4. Students need frequent and authentic interactions with words.

To build vocabulary knowledge, students need a minimum of four to twelve interactions with words to move from awareness of words to a definitional understanding (Allen, 2007; Allen & Landaker, 2005; Marzano, 2004; Stahl & Nagy, 2006). If your goal is for students to have a complex understanding of word meanings, then you have to provide frequent and purposeful vocabulary exposures throughout each instructional unit. Furthermore, the teaching of words must be accompanied by the reading of content texts and opportunities to build comprehension strategies for academic achievement to be maximized (Stahl & Nagy, 2006). Students need opportunities to interact with words in context and in difficult texts, such as primary sources and other informational texts found in social studies classes.

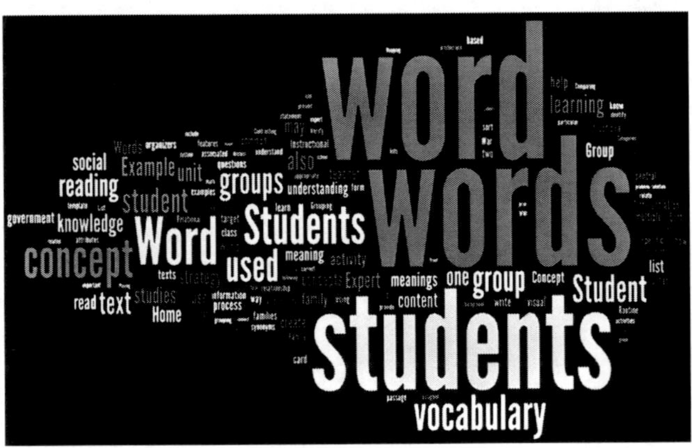

We know that words represent concepts and that concept understanding is central to critical thinking in social studies and in other content areas. Thus, vocabulary learning becomes a foundation for achieving Standard 10 of the Common Core State Standards for English/Language Arts:

> By the time students complete high school, they must be able to read and comprehend independently and proficiently the kinds of complex texts commonly found in college and careers.

ELA Common Core State Standard 10 is the reading standard for grade-specific text complexity demands as students progress in the sophistication of both what they read and the strategies they employ for comprehension. ELA expectations increase with each grade level, with the culminating expectation for high school graduates to be college and workforce ready. To achieve this standard by 12th grade, students must be proficient at independently reading and comprehending literature, informational texts, history/ social studies texts, as well as science and technology texts. The ELA Common Core State Standards further recommend that of students' required reading in school, 70% should be informational texts which is an increase of 15% over the types of texts students are expected to read in 8th grade. By 12th grade, 80% of all texts students read should exercise the communicative purposes of persuasion or explanation. For more information see, http://www.corestandards.org/assets/CCSSI_ELA%20Standards.pdf.

Vocabulary learning through reading primary source texts in social studies classes requires students to decipher facts (word information) related to the 5 W's and H (who, what, when, where, why, and how) that are the central attributes of a historical event. Readers also have to verify the authenticity of the source and the contextual factors that would have influenced the author's purpose. This process of historical thinking, learned and reinforced in social studies classes, models foundational thinking skills, word learning strategies, and concept building skills required for comprehending complex genres of text that align with ELA Common Core State Standards. As a result, student comprehension and literacy skills are supported through concept-based word learning and reading of informational texts frequently used in secondary social studies (Hiebert, 2011).

◉ The Academic Task

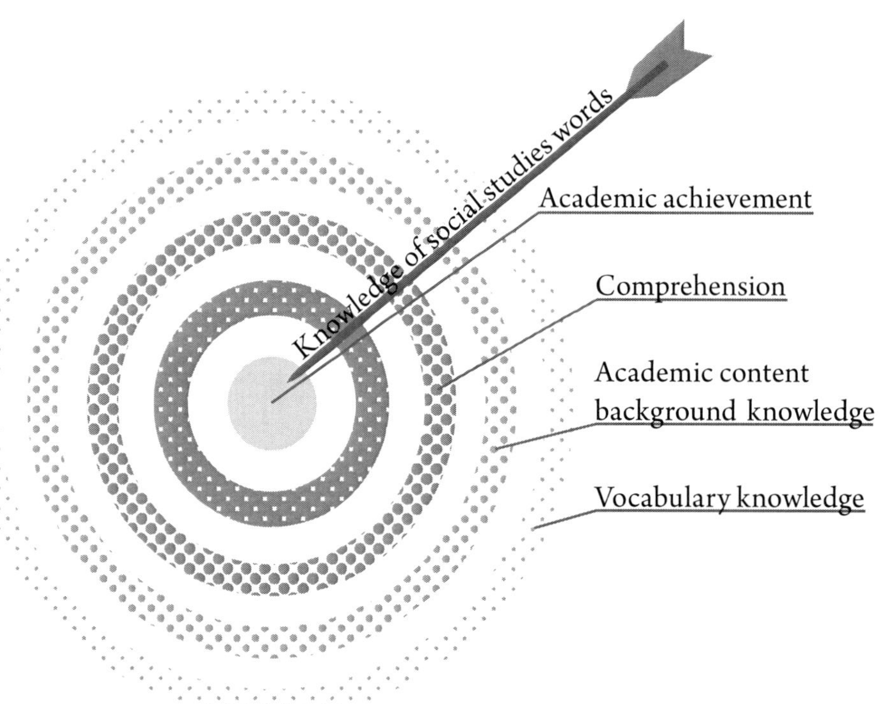

Our task, then, is to help students learn vocabulary so that they can understand what they read and learn in social studies classes. This is no simple task. The experiential knowledge of students varies greatly, depending on students' familiarity with social studies topics and on whether their educational experiences differ from the norm (Epstein, 2009; Ogle, Klemp, & McBride, 2007), such as cultural differences for non-native and immigrant students (Cruz & Thornton, 2009) or socioeconomic status (Marzano, 2004). Gaps in contextually-based academic knowledge create learning inequalities that are recognizable in the social stratification of knowledge and variance in student access to curriculum (Marzano, 2004; Pace, 2011). Thus, the changing dynamics of schools and the increased diversity among student populations presents new challenges for social studies teachers.

The Instructional Task: To Learn Vocabulary to Understand Informational Texts in Social Studies

No simple task

Student Challenges	**Social Studies Challenges**
Rising immigrant population	**Overloaded curriculum**
• Increasing first-generation students in American schools • Culturally different experiences and content learning	• Composite of diverse social science disciplines • Content area has independently recognizable academic language

Vocabulary Challenges

Overwhelming word learning expectations in high school

An even greater challenge to building social studies vocabulary is the complexity of the discipline itself. Social studies is by nature an overloaded curriculum (Bailey, 2007; Ogle, Klemp, & McBride, 2007; Resnick, 2006; Yarbrough, 2007). The area of social studies is a composite of diverse social science disciplines, including economics, history, geography, civics, political science, anthropology, sociology, psychology, and archaeology. Each content area has its own academic language and vocabulary, such as *equilibrium price, supply and demand, ex post facto, unconstitutional, judicial review, treaty, alliance, monarchy, nationalism, latitude and longitude, urbanization, deforestation, culture, identity, cognitive, egocentric, radiocarbon dating, knapping,* and so on. On average, students encounter more than six hundred discipline-specific words in one secondary social studies course alone (Bailey, 2007). Given that most states require multiple high school social studies courses, the task of learning as many as 2,400 social studies-specific words by high school graduation is overwhelming. This is even more problematic for struggling learners and English Language Learners (ELLs) who are challenged by culturally different word meanings and are unfamiliar with content-specific words in a spirally oriented, multi-grade social studies curriculum.

Content-based readings, in which complex vocabulary are found, further complicate learning. Social studies texts include multi-genre primary and secondary sources, such as maps, laws, letters, documents, court decisions, governmental policies, historical narratives, political cartoons, research briefs, propaganda posters, and more. Historical texts and primary sources may contain antiquated language and words that have changed meanings over time or are no longer used, making vocabulary even more convoluted. In addition, social studies written sources and texts, including tertiary sources (e.g., textbooks), present unique text arrangements and features, such as cause-and-effect structure overlaying a sequential text structure or a categorically organized framework of content (Massey & Heafner, 2004). Furthermore, textbooks are inherently difficult to decipher. Reading levels of textbooks often exceed by as much as two to four grade levels the reading abilities of the students using the text (Guthrie, 2008; Yarbrough, 2007) and this issue is compounded for English Language Learners (Cruz & Thornton, 2010). The overuse of images such as photographs, charts, maps, and graphs often inhibits rather than supports academic comprehension, making the social studies textbook even more challenging to understand (Ogle, Klemp, & McBride, 2007). The inability of struggling learners to successfully negotiate the complicated and complex organization of social studies texts is accelerated by the lack of background content knowledge that students bring to the content area (Allen & Landaker, 2005; Antunez, 2002; Marzano, 2004) making social studies one of the most challenging subjects to learn in high school.

As Nagy and Hiebert (2010) urge, for students whose exposure to the language of social studies occurs almost exclusively in the school context, the instructional choices that are made from the tens of thousands of words in social studies curriculum will determine the extent to which those students acquire the vocabulary needed for comprehending academic texts. Regretfully, in an attempt to expose students to exclusive content vocabulary, social studies courses become word factories that promote an overuse of short-term memorization strategies. More common than not, students are presented with unit-based word lists that are randomly or alphabetically organized, and they are expected to independently learn these words before the unit assessment (Allen & Landaker, 2005; Marzano, 2004; Sargent & Olney, 2011; VanSledright, 2011).

Recently, we reviewed twelve state and local school system-adopted secondary social studies textbooks for U.S. history courses. We found that the average length of a commonly used high school history textbook is 1,052 pages and included a mean of more than 632 vocabulary words. To understand what this means for the average high school student, let's consider that U.S. history courses at the secondary level are typically organized as semester or term courses that span eighteen weeks. Students would have to learn approximately 9 words each weekday and read, on average, 15 pages a night for four nights each week to complete the text and learn all terms in a semester. While this may not at first be overwhelming, let's take into account that students typically enroll in four classes each term; thus, these figures could be magnified fourfold.

The prospect of learning 36 words a night in four unrelated subjects is daunting and not feasible. Therefore, it is essential for educators to have a principled basis for identifying the words to target for social studies vocabulary instruction.

◎ Targeted Vocabulary Instruction

Navigating dense, content-laden social studies texts can be overwhelming even for good, much less struggling, adolescent readers with weak vocabularies. Comprehension derived from a rich vocabulary base requires more than definitional learning or phonetic usage; it demands understanding of discipline-specific word meanings in authentic reading and visual contexts. Proficient use of, and control over, the academic language of social studies becomes central to student learning of this multifaceted content area. Consequently, vocabulary development poses one of the greatest challenges to social studies instruction, because to read fluently and comprehend what is written, students need to use both phonics and context, as well as discipline-specific word knowledge (Allen & Landaker, 2005; Allen, 2007; Antunez, 2002; Marzano, 2004; Stahl and Nagy, 2006). Moreover, vocabulary learning must be purposefully and consistently reinforced through scaffolded instructional interventions.

In this curriculum, we recommend strategies for targeting student vocabulary learning for the purpose of improving student academic content comprehension. We emphasize teaching vocabulary not as isolated terms but as words to be integrated frequently throughout instructional units and as components of broader concepts. To improve student academic achievement, we present five instructional routines for teaching vocabulary in social studies:

1. Grouping and Organizing

2. Mapping and Visualizing

3. Comparing and Contrasting

4. Defining and Associating

5. Reviewing and Playing

The emphasis in each instructional routine is how the words function as parts of a whole concept. Approaching vocabulary through concept-based, contextually driven understanding improves student vocabulary acquisition. From vocabulary research we know that when students learn words in authentic contexts, they are more likely to remember and understand words they are reading (Allen & Landaker, 2005; Allen, 2007; Marzano, 2004; Stahl & Nagy, 2006). Making connections between words, comprehension, and academic content is the theoretical framework for this book.

Each instructional routine has a specific learning process that builds student word awareness and understanding in social studies through targeted vocabulary interventions. For example, while the fourth application, Defining and Connecting, emphasizes individual words, we purposely placed defining as the next-to-last learning application so that students experience the words as connected to other words, working from the macro level of the topic down to the micro level of the word. In addition, we model practical social studies applications of each instructional routine as we share specific content applications of various vocabulary strategies for secondary learners.

5 Instructional Routines: More Than Words

Concept-based, Contextually Driven, Social Studies Vocabulary Instruction

Reviewing and Playing

Defining and Associating

Comparing and Contrasting

Mapping and Visualizing

Grouping and Organizing

Another Vocabulary Approach?

Teachers have long recognized the importance of vocabulary instruction for learning social studies content. What's different about the *Targeted Vocabulary Approach*? First of all, we emphasize teaching vocabulary as the teaching of concepts, not just words. This moves vocabulary instruction from a list of words and definitions to be memorized to a critical thinking task. Second, instead of presenting a list of activities, the *Targeted Vocabulary Approach* presents five instructional routines. These routines organize activities into linked categories, reinforcing particular patterns of thinking such as creating connections and images. These routines support comprehension strategies for reading. Further, the instructional routines help streamline the teacher's planning process by creating a logical sequence of vocabulary instruction. Additionally, the activities suggested in the routines offer specific options for differentiating the learning in order to meet diverse student needs. Finally, the *Targeted Vocabulary Approach* offers a logical framework for providing students with the multiple exposures to vocabulary that are needed for deeper learning. The five routines suggest different ways of thinking about the words, while the variety of specific activities within each routine offer choice and variety for students and teachers.

◎ Using This Guide

For each instructional application, we offer a brief rationale, followed by multiple vocabulary teaching activities that you can use to support the instructional routine. You do not need to follow these strategies within each routine in every unit of study; rather, we offer them as various examples of how the instructional routine could be applied. Select the strategies in each routine that fit best with your instructional purpose, unit content, and student skills.

The materials in this curriculum provide content-specific, conceptual approaches to vocabulary instruction. The questions provided will help you guide students in discovery of relationships and word meanings. These comprehension questions define the word learning focus for each instructional routine. They are designed to help move vocabulary work away from being a memory task and toward a systematic approach to word learning. Questions provide focus for student word learning and your strategy usage.

As you apply strategies in each instructional routine, direct students to make connections to prior knowledge. Linking existing schema to new words through inductive and deductive thinking at various stages in the learning process will support academic vocabulary development. Inductive thinking moves student learning from specific words to broad generalizations, while deductive reasoning narrows generalizations to specific words. Combining the two will help students develop multiple pathways to word and concept learning.

The vocabulary interventions provided here draw on many existing resources and include new ways of thinking about and using these methods. You will also find that the strategies are purposefully used at strategic points in word learning. Early interventions in the first instructional routine build word awareness, while definitional word development occurs in the third and fourth instructional routines. The sequential process scaffolds the types of word exposures to maximize vocabulary learning.

Content uses are presented in each instructional routine to demonstrate how strategies can be applied with secondary social studies. Following the descriptions of the five instructional routines is an outline for using the routines in a high school social studies unit. The sample unit is on World Religions, which can be part of either a world history or world studies curriculum. It presents a holistic understanding for how the Targeted Vocabulary Approach can be used in your classroom. Remember the key to successful application of this approach is provide multiple and purposeful word exposures through the five tiered, sequential instructional routines.

INSTRUCTIONAL ROUTINE 1: GROUPING AND ORGANIZING

Applications

1. To identify word part patterns

2. To sort lists into categories and labels

3. To connect words to concepts

4. To relate word groups and organization to reading

Grouping is an application that is most useful as a preliminary activity to introduce students to concepts and words in relation to one another. Grouping does not provide students with detailed knowledge of unknown words, but it does help them identify words they might not know and how those words fit under a concept. Grouping is an inductive process whereby students draw on prior knowledge and begin to make connections to new learning. Ultimately, grouping words helps students build a foundation of word awareness that will support students as they read, encounter new words, and add to word groups. This later step bolsters students' relational understanding and enables concept formation.

Organizing is a comprehension process that students use to link words to concepts. In this stage of word learning, students move from grouping words to naming groups based on commonalities. This requires a more sophisticated level of word awareness. Students must not only recognize a word, but they must also link word groups to concepts. To be able to make these connections students will need a basic definitional knowledge of words. Through organizing, students develop their own knowledge of words and concepts through interactions with word meanings.

This first Instructional Routine, *Grouping and Organizing*, also serves as an initial assessment of students' knowledge of a concept. When students complete the following activities, you can easily identify those students who are familiar with the concept and individual words as well as those who are less familiar and have less background knowledge. This allows you to differentiate word learning as needed.

Grouping and Organizing skills can be applied to these skills: a) identify word part patterns, b) sort word lists into categories and labels, c) connect words to concepts and topics, and d) relate word groups and word organization to reading.

As students group and organize words, ask these vocabulary comprehension questions to focus student word learning:

1. How are words alike? Specifically, what word part patterns have you identified?

2. How can words be grouped? What labels describe word groups?

3. How do your word organizations relate to the overall concept we're studying?

4. How do words relate to what you are reading? What other words in the reading that we haven't listed might fit in the groups you've created?

◎ Application 1: Identify Word Part Patterns

Where do words come from? When and how were these words created? Do word meanings change? Do words mean the same today that they did when they were first invented? Do words have patterns or similar parts? Do these word parts have a common meaning? What are the origins of these word roots? The answers to these questions can be found in etymology, the study of the historical origins of words, word roots, and how words evolved. This process of exploring word part patterns is a preparatory academic vocabulary intervention and promotes generative word learning. With scaffolding you will guide students in the creation of word narratives that will unravel word meanings through discipline-specific skills.

Raising student awareness of word parts and word origins will increase reading comprehension and overall understanding of social studies. The following strategies give students the opportunity to explore common word patterns used in social studies texts. The purpose of these strategies is to help students understand meanings of common prefixes, suffixes, and root words used in social science disciplines. You can use these types of activities briefly at the beginning or end of class as a pre-reading strategy. It is an effective strategy to use when you introduce new words to students.

Words Are All Greek to Me

When students first encounter social studies vocabulary, words all too often appear Greek to them. The phrase "It's all Greek to me" means that something is totally incomprehensible. It comes from the Medieval Latin phrase "Graecum est; non potest legi" which translates as, "It is Greek; it cannot be read." The purpose of this generative vocabulary strategy is to make the unknown familiar by unpacking word meanings through word part patterns, word roots and word origins. *Words Are All Greek to Me* also draws upon the rich influence of Ancient civilizations and European languages in inventing word meanings used in American culture. You can use this strategy when first introducing words or as a pre-reading activity. Through repetition of this process, students will improve word recognition and become more secure in generating their own meanings for words. This activity aligns with National Council for the Social Studies National Standard 2: Time, Continuity, and Change. Students learn words in a historical sense and explore the continuity and change of word meanings over time. Procedural steps describe the process of *Words Are All Greek to Me* and will guide your implementation. To guide you in your application of the strategy, a content example follows.

To implement this strategy, follow these steps:

Step 1: Sort Words

1. Give students a randomized list of frequently used social studies words that have a common pattern.

2. Have students sort words into groups based on word part patterns they have observed.

Step 2: Label Patterns

1. Together, you and your students identify the base word or word part by underlining or highlighting word patterns.

2. Have students label the word part, such as, Greek word parts *-crat/-cracy* and *-arch/-archy*. This organizational grouping ends with words aligned vertically in columns.

3. Together, you and your students pause to discuss grouping strategies and explore possible meanings of word parts.

Step 3: Identify Commonalities in Words

1. Students match the base word with derived forms to align common words horizontally (e.g., rows of words that share similarities in meaning).

2. Discuss with students possible meanings of the word groups. Have them explore word group similarities and differences. Then ask them to hypothesize about differences and possible word meanings.

Step 4: Generalize Word Part Meanings

1. Have students generalize word part meanings. Guide them to explore whether word part meanings change or remain the same in the various forms.

2. Finally, you and your students formalize word part definitions.

Web Tools

The following Web sites offer additional ways for students to explore Greek word parts:

*   For an additional list of *-cracy* words, see
    http://phrontistery.info/govern.html

*   For additional definitions, see the CIA Factbook at
    https://www.cia.gov/library/publications/the-world-factbook/docs/notesanddefs.html

*   For Greek root words, see the Etymology Dictionary at
    http://www.etymonline.com/

*   For a game to test knowledge of root words, see "It's Greek to Me" at
    http://teacher.scholastic.com/activities/athens_games/gamegreektome.htm

Example: Words Are All Greek to Me—Greek Roots

Random Word List

monarchy	theocrat	democrat	plutocrat
matriarch	autocrat	patriarchy	bureaucrat
hierarchy	theocracy	oligarchy	anarchy
technocrat	anarchist	plutocracy	aristocracy
democracy	aristocrat	matriarchy	hierarchical
patriarch	technocracy	bureaucracy	monarch
autocracy		oligarch	

Step 1: Sort Words (Vertical Order)

Group A	Group B	Group C	Group D
theocracy	theocrat	monarchy	matriarch
plutocracy	democrat	patriarchy	anarchist
aristocracy	plutocrat	hierarchy	hierarchical
aristocracy	autocrat	oligarchy	patriarch
democracy	bureaucrat	anarchy	monarch
technocracy	technocrat	matriarchy	oligarch
bureaucracy	aristocrat		
autocracy			

Step 2: Identify Word Part Patterns

Group A	Group B	Group C	Group D
theo*cracy*	theo*crat*	mon*archy*	matri*arch*
pluto*cracy*	demo*crat*	patri*archy*	an*archist*
aristo*cracy*	pluto*crat*	hier*archy*	hier*arch*ical
aristo*cracy*	auto*crat*	olig*archy*	patri*arch*
demo*cracy*	bureau*crat*	an*archy*	mon*arch*
techno*cracy*	techno*crat*	matri*archy*	olig*arch*
bureau*cracy*	aristo*crat*		
auto*cracy*			

Label Groups

-cracy	-crat	-archy	-arch-
theo*cracy*	theo*crat*	mon*archy*	matri*arch*
pluto*cracy*	demo*crat*	patri*archy*	an*archist*
aristo*cracy*	pluto*crat*	hier*archy*	hier*arch*ical
aristo*cracy*	auto*crat*	olig*archy*	patri*arch*
demo*cracy*	bureau*crat*	an*archy*	mon*arch*
techno*cracy*	techno*crat*	matri*archy*	olig*arch*
bureau*cracy*	aristo*crat*		
auto*cracy*			

Step 3: Sort by Word Similarities (Horizontal Order)

-cracy	-crat	-archy	-arch-
democracy	democrat	monarchy	monarch
aristocracy	aristocrat	oligarchy	oligarch
plutocracy	plutocrat	anarchy	anarchist
aristocracy	aristocrat	hierarchy	hierarchical
bureaucracy	bureaucrat	matriarchy	matriarch
technocracy	technocrat	patriarchy	patriarch
theocracy	theocrat		
autocracy	autocrat		

Define Word Parts

-cracy	-crat	-archy	-arch-
democracy	democrat	monarchy	monarch
aristocracy	aristocrat	oligarchy	oligarch
plutocracy	plutocrat	anarchy	anarchist
aristocracy	aristocrat	hierarchy	hierarchical
bureaucracy	bureaucrat	matriarchy	matriarch
technocracy	technocrat	patriarchy	patriarch
theocracy	theocrat		
autocracy	autocrat		
power, government	**ruler**	**rule, rulership**	**ruler, chief**

Step 4: Generalize Meanings of Word Parts

-crat/-cracy means "power, rule, or government"

-archy also means "rule" and is used when a noun ends in *-arch*

-arch means "government, ruler, or chief"

-ment means "to be ruled over"

There is a difference between the suffix *-archy,* meaning "rulership," and *-cracy,* meaning "power," which both come from Greek roots. Follow up with individual word meanings and Greek roots.

Democracy	Monarchy	Oligarchy	Aristocracy
demos = common people, district *-cracy* = rule, strength, rule or government by, power Origin: Greek demokratia = popular government Definition: government by the people	*mono* = single, alone, one *-cracy* = rule, strength, rule or government by, power Origin: Greek monarkhia = absolute rule Definition: government or absolute rule by one person	*oligoi* = few, small, little *-cracy* = rule, strength, rule or government by, power Origin: Greek oligarkhia = government by the few Definition: government by the few	*aristo* = best *ar* = to fit together *isto* = most fitting *-cracy* = rule, strength, rule or government by Origin: Greek aristokratia = government or rule of the best Definition: government by the best citizens or the privileged class

Grouping and Organizing Suffix Word Patterns

Utilizing word roots allows students to recognize organizational patterns that reoccur in social studies texts. When the process of *Words Are All Greek to Me* is applied to suffixes, you can begin to build student word recognition and relational thinking. *Grouping and Organizing Suffix Word Patterns* draws upon the notion that most social studies texts, especially those used in history courses, present information categorically. To comprehend these texts, students need to be able to identify the 5Ws&H (Questions: Who? What? When? Where? Why? and How?). Suffix word patterns provide contextual clues that students can use to answer the 5Ws&H. Students will not only be able to group words based on suffixes, they will begin to form word meanings based on these patterns. Using the strategy of *Grouping and Organizing Suffix Word Patterns* early in the academic year will produce generative word learning and heightened word awareness. Early applications will require your direction, but as students become familiar with suffixes students will be able to integrate this word building process into their daily reading.

You can apply the same process you used with students in *Words Are All Greek to Me* to suffixes, such as, *-ism*, *-ist*, and *-ize*. These are commonly used suffixes in social studies texts. You can find other suffix lists online (e.g. http://www.michigan-proficiency-exams.com/suffix-list.html). The same steps for this activity would be replicated as described above. However, be aware that there may be nuanced differences in meaning between words with the same suffix (as is evident in the *-ize* column in the following example). Remember the purpose for using *Grouping and Organizing Suffix Word Patterns* is to have students think categorically about words as they encounter new words in informational and explanatory texts.

Example: Grouping and Organizing Suffix Word Patterns (-ism, -ist, and -ize)

The following example lists words with the suffixes *-ism, -ist,* and *-ize*. After showing students the list, you would provide the definitions of the three suffixes:

- *-ism:* belief in or indicating a doctrine, system, or body of principles and practices

- *-ist:* one who believes

- *-ize:* to convert into or to subject to

-ism	-ist	-ize
capitalism	capitalist	capitalize
communism	communist	communize
fascism	fascist	-
socialism	socialist	socialize
terrorism	terrorist	terrorize
authoritarianism	authoritarian	-
totalitarianism	totalitarian	totalitarianize
anarchism	anarchist	anarchize
spiritualism	spiritualist	spiritualize
federalism	federalist	federalize
egalitarianism	egalitarian	equalize
centralism	centralist	centralize
absolutism	absolutist	-
despotism	despot	despotize
utilitarianism	utilitarian	-
feminism	feminist	feminize

Next, launch a discussion as to why some words have *-ism, -ist,* and *-ize* suffixes and others do not. Are there similar words (such as *equalize*) that have common meanings for the suffixes? It is important for students to discuss how the meanings of *-ize* words change slightly from the other two columns. Have students create more sophisticated and generalizable definitions of each suffix, such as, *-ist* means "a person who adheres to a certain doctrine, custom, practice, or is characterized by a trait or action." Then have students indentify commonalities of how *-ist* characterizes the words in that column. You can further challenge student suffix word learning by introducing new words with similar suffixes, like, feminist or anarchist. The goal is to have students develop word part recognition as a way for students to generate word meanings.

An additional step to this activity is to have students categorize *-ism, -ist,* and *-ize* based on the 5WQs. To explain the learning outcomes of this process, consider that a student is reading and encounters descriptions of early 20th Century women Emma Goldman or Susan B. Anthony. The descriptive words are feminist and anarchist. The student should initially recognize the common suffix *-ist*. Next, the student links the suffix to a generalizable definition, such as, *-ist* means "a person who adheres to a certain doctrine, custom, practice, or is characterized by a trait or action." From the suffix, the student will be able to group both women as important people who would have been characterized by a common trait (gender) and who were involved in a social movement for change (anarchy means without government). Next you would ask the student focus questions to promote a higher level of relational word learning. Some questions might include: What movement would be classified as both feminist and anarchist? Why would a feminist also be called an anarchist? Using these questions, you could then have students explore word definitions and root word meanings using etymologies. Interestingly, both anarchist and feminist have Greek and French word origins.

As you are implementing this strategy, you will want to determine the following:

1. First, you want to see that students recognize *-ism*, *-ist*, and *-ize* as common suffixes. This is demonstrated when they can group the words into appropriate categories.

2. Second, you want to see that students can use the suffix patterns to generate meanings for each of the suffixes. This is demonstrated from student discussion or by asking them to write down definitions.

3. Third, you want to extend students' understanding by asking them to discuss why some words do not have an *-ize* form of the word. This is demonstrated from student discussion or by asking them to write a written reflection.

4. Fourth, you provide discussion about the nuances of the meanings.

5. Fifth, you ask students to apply their knowledge to a new word.

Example: Grouping and Organizing Capitalism Suffix Word Patterns (-ism, -ist, and -ize)

This example provides a different format for how you might guide students in exploring word origin and word part patterns. To use this strategy, you would give students the word *Capitalism* and the following template.

Concept	Capitalism				
Actions	Word Origins	Root Word	**Suffix**		
			-ism	-ize	-ists
Explanation	Historical beginnings	Originating word			
Word			Capitalism		
Word Meaning					
Definition					

Next, students fill in the missing information and formulate their own definition of the focus word. This modification presents a targeted approach to concept development rather than the more generalized approach described in the previous application. This strategy is best used after words have been introduced as an activity to promote a higher level of word awareness.

Concept	Capitalism				
Actions	Word Origins	Root Word	Suffix		
			-ism	-ize	-ists
Explanation	Historical beginnings	Originating word	an action, state or condition, principles or doctrines of the root word	To cause to become, change into, to affect, to subject to	Person or people who practice or ar concerned with certain principles and/or doctrines
Word	capitalis, capit, caput	Capital	Capitalism	Capitalize	Capitalists
Word Meaning	of the head stem of head	accumu-lation of wealth, prof-it, power, assets	Economic system characterized by private ownership, supply and demand principles, and equilibrium prices and free markets	By profit, exploit, utilize, to take advantage of	Group or class distinguished from labors
Definition	Capitalism is the accumulation of wealth, profit, power, and assets.				

◎ Application 2: Sort Word Lists

Categories and Labels

When presenting students with word lists at the beginning of an instructional unit, use *Categories and Labels* as a method for helping students understand why these words were selected. Students will begin to understand relationships among words as they organize words into meaningful groups. This inductive process will help students identify common features among word groups. They will explore word meanings as they unpack how words can be organized. *Categories and Labels* is a useful strategy to assess or build background knowledge about a concept or unit topic. It may also be beneficial in supporting students in defining attributes of words and determining how words relate to one another and the central concept or main topic. *Categories and Labels* is also a very effective strategy for supporting higher cognitive skills when used to introduce an instructional unit word list. Students must anticipate word categories, predict and verify word meanings, and hypothesize what the unit is about based on the given word list. To implement this strategy, follow these steps:

1. Provide each student with a blank template and list of words for the unit.

To address the needs of all learners:

- You can present words on *Vocabulary Manipulative Cards* (*VMCs*) or on sticky notes. *VMCs* work like flash cards with words on one side of the card. *VMCs* are explained in more detail later in the book.

- *VMCs* can include word meaning clues, such as brief texts using words, iconic images that represent words, symbolic drawings or word pictures, photos, or other visual examples. You can also include definitions, but visual resources are more effective in supporting early word learning.

- When working with English Language Learners (ELLs), you can create *VMCs* with word translations to support linguistic word learning.

2. Read aloud the words and remind students where they can access resources to assist in determining word meanings if you are not providing these as visual cues.

Example: Vocabulary Manipulative Cards (VMCs)

3. Students then work in small groups to sort words.

   To address the needs of all learners, including English Language Learners, and learners with special needs, *VMCs* can be used in varied formats.

   - For students who need a more tactile activity, *VMCs* allow students to sort words physically.

   - For students who need a more visual activity, *VMCs* with symbolic images can be used.

   - For students who need linguistic support, *VMCs* can include native language word equivalents and culturally meaningful images.

4. Students collaboratively categorize words into word families. During the process, students discuss word attributes that they used to group the words.

5. Students assign labels to each group, thus naming the common features of organized groups. If students struggle to determine categories and labels, you could provide the labels and ask students to sort the words under each label.

6. Students justify in writing their selection of groups and the placement of each word under a label by using the final row of the chart to describe common features or meanings of the category.

Differentiated Outcomes: An additional step for *Categories and Labels* is to have students create an outline using the categories as headings and subheadings and then identify the unit topic. This would be a good way to introduce a text reading or unit outline to guided or double entry notes.

Differentiated Applications: A variation of when to apply this strategy would be to have students sort all of the words from their personal *Word Wall* (a method described later) at various points in the unit. Sorting words that they have already sorted while adding new words can provide valuable review as well as help students see new ways of sorting previous words.

Categories and Labels Template

Categories and Labels				
Sorted Words				
Define Common Features and Attributes				

Word List, Group, Label, Add, Sequence, Outline, Title

Sequencing groups of word families in a logical order creates a meaningful progression in vocabulary development. You do this intuitively, yet rarely do students think about sequential word learning. A typical ordering of words within word families will move from more familiar words to unknown words. Sequencing of word families will vary based on content familiarity and how a concept or topic is conceptualized. One strategy you can use for this process is *Word List, Group, Label, Add, Sequence, Outline, Title.* To implement this strategy, follow these steps:

1. Provide a word list to students.

2. Have students create groups of words based on the attributes words shared in common.

3. Next, students label groups by using a word that best describes why these words are organized together. These groups become *word families* to demonstrate connections among words and how words relate to the concept.

4. Students can add words that are missing in each word family group. These are essential vocabulary words that students need to know to understand group and concept meanings. Your help may be needed in this step.

5. Students will then sequence groups of word families in a logical order that creates a meaningful progression in vocabulary development. Sequencing will vary based on content and how the students perceive the concept. There may also be an ordering of words within word families that move from more familiar words to unknown words. You may need to direct students in this process.

6. From the completed chart, students create an outline and give the outline a title. The title becomes the prediction of what these words mean collectively. It is also a meaningful step when students are hypothesizing about the unit concept. If students struggle with titles, you can offer suggestions to guide their thinking.

Word List, Group, Label, Add, Sequence, Outline, Title Template

Sequencing				
Categories and Labels				
Sorted Words				
Added Words				

Political and Economic Systems

Word List	Word List, Group, Label, Add, Sequence
Government, Anarchy, Dictatorship, Commonwealth, Federalism, Confederacy, Communism, Socialism, Totalitarianism, Fascism, Democracy, Aristocracy, Matriarchy, Oligarchy, Bureaucracy, Patriarchy, Plutocracy, Authoritarianism, Capitalism, Republic, Revolution, Constitutional Monarch, Absolutism, Direct Democracy, Tyranny, Theocracy, Autonomy, Imperialism	**Types of Governments:** Dictatorship, monarchy, oligarchy, theocracy, socialism, communism, democracy, republic, confederacy, commonwealth, fascism **Control of Power [autonomy]:** Anarchy, Dictatorship, Commonwealth, Federalism, Confederacy, Totalitarianism, Aristocracy, Matriarchy, Bureaucracy, Patriarchy, Plutocracy, Authoritarianism, Capitalism, Republic **Divisions of Power [autonomy]:** Federal, state, local **Other:** Representatives, parliament, vote, political, liberal, power, revenue, state, govern, rule, law, revolution

◎ Application 3: Connect Words to Concepts

Learning to connect words to the central idea of the instructional unit builds word understanding. The central idea is usually a concept, such as revolution, but can be a specific topic like the American Revolution. Students organize words for the purpose of exploring the meaning of the central concept. This is a deductive thinking process whereby students move word lists to a generalized concept. This process requires a sophisticated level of word awareness and promotes relational thinking. Students must not only recognize a word but also connect word meanings and link word groups to a concept. Through organizing, students develop a generative understanding of words and create relational links to the concept.

Concept Trees

Concept Trees is a vocabulary strategy that uses the visual metaphor of a tree to give students an opportunity to see how words (leaves) connect to a central concept (tree trunk). Students draw these connections by grouping words into word families. The metaphor of family implies a relationship among words; thus, family names are derivatives of common attributes among word groups. Other metaphorical descriptions can be used when appropriately aligned with informational texts. Items such as rain, clouds, sunshine, roots, ground, etc., could be added. You can use *Concept Trees* as a review or as an assessment of students' word learning. It is also a very effective reading comprehension strategy and works well when used to teach students to recognize words in social studies texts. *Concept Trees* is a mnemonic device that provides various synaptic pathways to recall, remember, and comprehend information.

The diagram on the next page illustrates how *Concept Trees* are formed. To implement this strategy, follow these steps:

1. *List:* Provide students with a copy of the *Concept Trees* handout and the unit's word list.

2. *Predict:* Before going further, ask students to consider the word list and then create a list of questions that they predict will be answered in the text, or have them predict what the unit of study might be about.

3. *Read & Group:* Have students read the unit, organizing the leaves (words) on their handout as they read. To address the needs of all learners, you can create leaf *VMCs* for a more tactile and interactive activity. Additionally by having the words on each leaf, you can guide students in determining which words are important as they are reading the chapter. This modification scaffolds student comprehension and word recognition during reading.

4. *Name Word Families*: Guide students to give a name to each group of words and place a group in each of the provided boxes. You can have students create a name for leaf groups to create a word family or you can provide family name cards that can be used as manipulative.

5. *Identify Concept*: Students then give a title or name to the concept that ties all of the family word groups together.

6. *Answer & Verify:* With your direction, students should revisit their questions and predictions outlined in step 2. Have students answer the list of questions as a whole class or individually. Additionally, you will want to help students confirm and verify their predictions using the concept tree they created. This last step will give you the opportunity to further explain word meanings as well as information presented with the text reading.

7. *Write:* An extension of this activity is to have students write about the information presented in their *Concept Trees*. You and the students collectively develop a thesis statement and summary paragraph from the *Concept Trees* as a whole class. Students would then, independently or in writing partners, create a persuasive essay or narrative essay describing the significance of the concept using word families for organization structure and words as facts to support their argument. This step is optional.

You, the teacher (symbolized by the Sun), nurture and develop the concept tree pedagogical interventions to build vocabulary-oriented content-based instruction (rain).

CONCEPT TREES

Name ____   Date _____________________________

1. **Leaves (Word List):** ____

2. **Questions & Predictions:** ____

3. **Read & Group:** Organize the leaves.

Family 1:	Family 2:	Family 3:	Family 4:	Family 5:	Family 6:

4. **Name Word Families:** Put the leaves on the tree and name the family branches.

5. **Identify the Concept Tree:** ____

6. **Answer & Verify:** ____

____

____

____

____

Middle Concept

Another strategy for connecting word learning to concepts text is *Middle Concept.* The objective of this strategy is to give students vocabulary words before reading and ask them to predict the middle concept. You can use this strategy both to develop conceptual thinking about content vocabulary and as an assessment of these skills. To implement this strategy, follow these steps:

1. Present students with a short word list. All words should relate to a single concept.

2. Using a concept map, visually identify a relationship between three or four words. You will need to display your center concept diagram to the whole class. You can give students blank copies of the concept map or you can have students draw this diagram.

3. Begin by writing each of the words in one of the smaller circles.

4. Ask students to supply the concept that links each of the words and write it in the middle circle.

5. After students understand the process of linking the words and concepts, begin leaving out both the central concept and one of the words.

6. Ask students to fill in the missing word and the central concept.

7. Ask students to explain the relationship of words to the middle concept using a Think-Pair-Share discussion model or in a written statement.

8. In the final step, asking students to read a passage to verify the accuracy of the middle concept and add any missing words.

9. After reading, students affirm their learning by explaining how the words are connected to the central concept. Review why each word is important.

Differentiated Processes:

- In a variation of this strategy, you or the students select four words from the vocabulary list. Then students free-write all that they know about the words. This modification serves as a diagnostic assessment of student prior knowledge and will help you determine what information needs to be emphasized.

- Another way to modify this strategy is for you to place four words in the circle while the student shades or colors the word that does not belong and then writes an explanation for the choice. The ability to recognize inaccurate or misinformation is a high-order thinking skill and one that promotes sophisticated word learning.

Example: Middle Concept

Word Family: Thirteenth Amendment, Fourteenth Amendment, Fifteenth Amendment, Civil Rights Act of 1964, Economic Opportunity Act of 1964, Voting Rights Act of 1965, Twenty-fourth Amendment

Central Idea or Category Label: Legislative acts

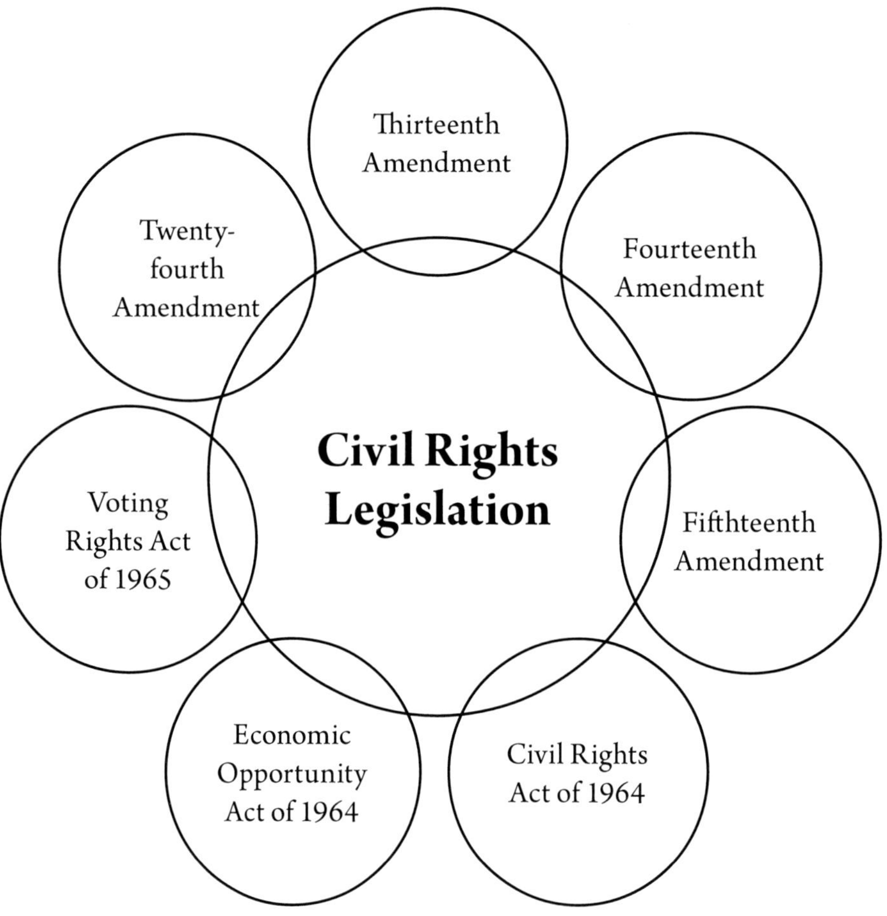

In your own words, explain how the words are related to the central concept:

Each of these legislative acts provided the expansion and protection of the civil liberties of minority groups in America. They were central forces in forcing change for African Americans during the civil rights movement. Laws and the enactment of laws were necessary for change in discriminatory and segregation practices between the dominant race and minority races.

Note: This example was used as a whole class activity. The narrative is a teacher-directed collective explanation of the *Middle Concept.*

Example: Middle Concept Student Application

A student application of *Middle Concept* illustrates a variation of the concept map. In this example, the student wrote the following: philosopher name, ideas of that thinker, and personal meanings of each enlightenment belief. The student summarized the middle concept through writing.

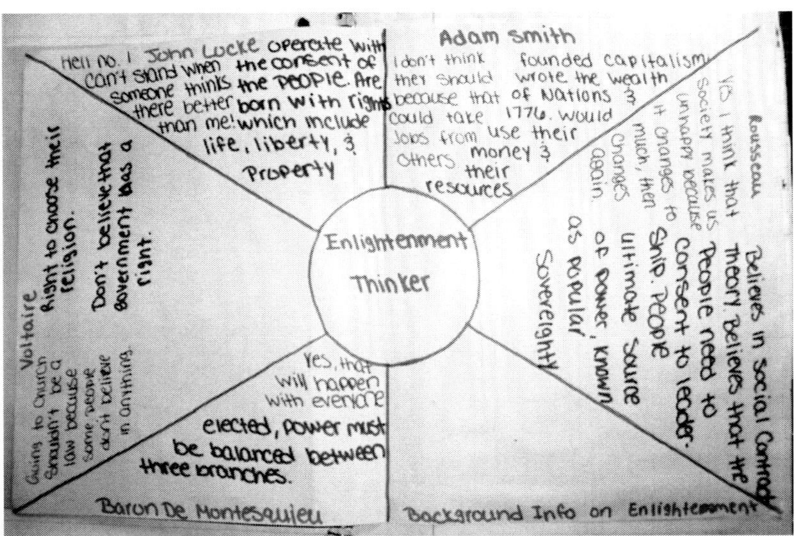

In your own words, explain how the words are related to the central concept:

Enlightenment means new ways of thinking. When our founding fathers decided to create our own government, they had to look to others for ideas. These enlightenment thinkers provided new ways of thinking about the relationship between people and their government. Life today would be very different without these ideas. We would all be beaten, homeless, or murdered. Even today some of these rights are abused and we take them for granted. That is why we need to remember the principles for which this country was founded. [Typed student written response.]

MIDDLE CONCEPT

Name ____   Date _______________________________

Directions: Identify the concept that links these words and explain how the words fit with the concept.

In your own words, explain how the words are related to the central concept:

____

____

____

____

____

◎ Application 4: Relate Word Groups and Organization to Reading

Connecting word learning to texts allows students to encounter words in context. It also supports generative word learning through authentic and multiple exposures. These activities are word grouping strategies that, when used as pre-reading activities, will enhance student comprehension of word meanings.

Degrees of Knowledge

Degrees of Knowledge, adapted from Allen (1999), Stahl & Nagy (2006), and Bear et al. (2008), is a good tool for encouraging students to self-assess their familiarity with words and for allowing you to evaluate words that will need specific vocabulary interventions. To implement this strategy, follow these steps:

1. Give students a list of target vocabulary for a given passage, chapter, or unit.

   To address the needs of all students, you could:

   - Read aloud target words to the whole class.

   - Read aloud target words and have students sort and spell the words.

2. Have students sort words based on their perceived knowledge of each word and its meaning. Students sort words based on these given categories:

   - I don't know it at all.

   - I have seen or heard it, but I don't know the meaning.

   - I think I know the meaning.

   - I know a meaning.

3. Ask students to read the assigned text and amend their initial sorted lists. As students read words in the passage, their level of familiarity with words will shift due to contextual learning of words. Students will move words among the columns for degrees of word knowledge.

4. After the reading, have students convene in small groups or as partners to share their knowledge and ideas regarding word meanings.

5. At the end of the unit, guide students to revisit their lists and amend them as necessary. Ask students to reflect on how their word knowledge changed over the course of the unit. Help students to recognize the sources of information that they found more helpful is supporting changes in their degrees of word knowledge.

HOW WELL DO I KNOW THESE WORDS?

Name ____   Date ___________________________

Directions: First, read the words at the bottom of the page silently. After you read each word, write it under the column heading that best describes what you know about the word.

I know a meaning.

I think I know the meaning.

I have seen or heard it, but I don't know the meaning.

I don't know it at all.

Degrees of Knowledge

Word List:

Example: Degrees of Knowledge—How Well Do I Know These Words?

I know a meaning.

- metropolitan area
- migration
- monolingual
- multilingual

I think I know the meaning.

- municipality
- microstate
- multinational state
- migration/international

I have seen or heard it, but I don't know the meaning.

- multiple nuclei model
- NAFTA
- metes and bounds
- Monotheism

I don't know it at all.

- Megapolis
- Mercator projection
- moraine
- MSA

Degrees of Knowledge

Word List:

- Megapolis
- Mercator projection
- Metes and bounds
- Metropolitan area
- Microstate
- migration
- migration/international
- monolingual
- Monotheism
- moraine
- MSA
- multilingual
- multinational state
- multiple nuclei model
- multistate nation
- municipality
- NAFTA

Predict the Pattern

You can use *Predict the Pattern* to preview key vocabulary at the beginning of a unit or as a during-reading activity to reinforce word meaning that is critical to comprehension. You can do this in one session, or you can make a running log of words, with the final steps being completed after students finish reading. The purpose of this activity is for students to be able to predict the meaning of a unit through grouping and organizing of words found in context. This learning outcome is achieved by having students link words found in text to content comprehension. Students are asked to develop a *gist statement* that summarizes the word categories created from the text reading. This is similar to a thesis sentence. It is a good exercise in building students' higher level thinking skills. Next, students are challenged to self-regulate their learning by figuring out what information they are going to need to know to clarify the placement of words and the gist statement. These *things to discover statements* guide students in examining missing information and determining how additional information can be found. To be able to complete this final step, students will have to be able to recognize both what they know and what they don't know as well as identify the necessary steps to ensure understanding. To implement this strategy, follow these steps:

1. Assign a reading passage from the current unit and distribute the template.

2. Have students read the passage. As they read, have them sort words into the appropriate category.

3. Have students write a *gist statement* that summarizes their findings.

4. Have student write *things to discover statements* that describe knowledge the student still needs to acquire to truly understand the reading passage and the related vocabulary.

5. Finally, ask students to identify the central concept or topic of the passage. You can modify the template to better relate to other content areas and to the specific reading selection. Category names could include groupings such as:

    - 5Ws&H: Who, What, When, Where, Why and How?, or

    - Location, Place, Human-Environment Interaction, Movement, Region.

Differentiated Process:

1. One variation involves giving students a word list before they read a passage.

2. Students then sort words into named categories that you give them based on their word knowledge.

3. Then students write a *gist statement* about the meaning of the word groups.

4. Students ask questions in which they identify what they will need to learn to understand the meaning of the word grouping and organization.

5. Students predict the title of the reading as an attempt to identify the central concept.

6. Then, students read the passage.

7. As they are reading, students verify their word sorts. They move words among groups as they encounter the meaning of the words in context.

8. After reading, students rewrite the *gist statement* based on their comprehension of the passage.

9. In the final step, students write new questions to clarify understanding.

Differentiated Outcomes:

- As an alternative, you can use this process over the course of a unit of study rather than in a lesson.

- As students read new passages and learn additional content, they verify word grouping and organization over time.

- The final product would be a good example of cumulative student learning.

PREDICT THE PATTERN

Name ____   Date _____________________________

Title of Reading: ____

What is the central concept or topic? ____

Directions: Sort the words into probable sections. Once you have sorted the words, write the *gist statement* and the *things to discover statements*.

List of words:

People	Places	Miscellaneous *(Use only when you don't know* *what the words mean.)*
Outcomes	**Conflicts**	**Gist statement…**

Things to discover *(based on what I need to know to clarify the placement of words and the gist statement)*

1.

2.

Example: World History Predict the Pattern

Title of Reading: <u>World History Textbook</u>

What is the central concept or topic?   <u>WWII</u>

Directions: Sort the words into probable sections. Once you have sorted the words, write the *gist statement* and the *things to discover statements.*

List of words:

- triangular trade
- turning point
- tribute
- tyranny
- Triple Alliance

- Triple Entente
- troubadours
- United Nations
- urban
- urbanization

- utilitarianism
- Vedic poetry
- Victor Emmanuel II
- Vikings
- Vladimir Lenin

- wage slavery
- Warsaw Pact
- Weimar Republic
- welfare state
- wheel

People	**Places**	**Miscellaneous** *(Use only when you don't know what the words mean.)*
troubadours Victor Emmanuel II Vikings Vladimir Lenin	Weimar Republic	urbanization utilitarianism Vedic poetry wheel
Outcomes	**Conflicts**	**Gist statement…**
triangular trade United Nations tribute Triple Alliances Triple Entente	turning point tyranny wage slavery	Alliances were very important leading up to war.

Things to discover (based on what I need to know to clarify the placement of words and the gist statement)

1.   How does "welfare state" relate to the other concepts?

2.   What constitutes a tribune?

3.   What were the forces behind the Warsaw Pact? Outcomes?

Example: Economics Unit Predict the Pattern

Title of Reading: <u>Economics Unit</u>

What is the central concept or topic? <u>Economic Systems</u>

Directions: Sort the words into probable sections. Once you have sorted the words, write the *gist statement* and the *things to discover statements.*

List of words:

Goods, services, complements, diminishing marginal utility, demand, substitutes, supply, profit, equilibrium price, surplus, shortage, price ceiling, production, free market economy, Adam Smith, laissez-faire, consumers, producers, wants, needs, scarcity, free enterprise, invisible hand, locational theory, purchasing power, net income, and gross income, bottom line, regulation, taxes, progressive, proportional and regressive taxes, EPA, Consumer Protection Agency, legislation, fiscal policy, GDP

People	**Consumer**	**Miscellaneous** *(Use only when you don't know what the words mean.)*
supply, profit, production, goods, advertising, production, substitutes, bottom line	demand, complements, law of diminishing marginal utility, wants, needs, price ceiling, purchasing power, net income, and gross income	locational theory, equilibrium price, laissez-faire
Government	**Marketplace Interaction**	**Gist statement…**
Regulation, taxes, progressive, proportional and regressive taxes, EPA, Consumer Protection Agency, legislation, fiscal policy, GDP	laissez-faire, shortage, surplus, price ceiling, Adam Smith, scarcity, invisible hand, free enterprise, free market economy	The interaction between producers and consumers with some governmental influence defines how the nation's human, natural, and capital resources are produced, managed, distributed, and consumed in the marketplace.

Things to discover (based on what I need to know to clarify the placement of words and the gist statement)

1. What is the difference between a market and command economy?

2. What role does the government play in a free market economy, specifically in the American economy?

3. Who controls resources?

4. How do consumers influence the marketplace?

Sort and Verify

You can use the *Sort and Verify* strategy before and during reading to reinforce content concepts and target vocabulary. This strategy serves as an assessment of prior knowledge, an organizer for student reading, and a comprehension strategy for later work. If you use *Vocabulary Manipulative Cards (VMCs)*, this can be a more engaging tactile method. There are three variations of *Sort and Verify:* the *Word Sort and Verify with* Insert strategy, the *Complete Word Sort and Verify* method, and *Sort and Verify Words in Context.*

Word Sort and Verify with Insert Strategy

1. To implement the *Word Sort and Verify with Insert* strategy, follow these steps:

2. Select words from two or three word families and present them in random order. The word families should be major section headings from the chosen text.

   Then, have students sort the words into word family groups. They may sort some of the words incorrectly. This is acceptable as a first attempt.

   To address the needs of all students:

   - You may supply the word family labels.

   - You can ask students to generate the word family labels.

3. Students complete the assigned text reading.

   As they read, students should verify that each word is under the correct word family heading by placing a check mark in front of the word. If the word is incorrectly placed, they should move it to the correct column. If they do not find the word in the reading, students should place a question mark in front of it.

Example: Word Sort and Verify with Insert Strategy

For this example, students were asked to sort words into the following four categories:

	Spain		Great Britain		France		Other
√	Conquistador	√	Cabot	√	Fur trade		

Here, the *Other* category would include those words that might fit under Dutch and Portuguese exploration. Students found the above words in the reading, so they placed check marks in front of the listed words. If they had found a word in the list that was not in the reading, they would have placed a question mark in front of it. In this format, you will be able to assess student prior knowledge of words, help students organize their reading, and scaffold student comprehension for future reading.

Complete Word Sort and Verify Method

To use the *Complete Word Sort and Verify* method, follow these steps:

1. Pre-select the vocabulary words and strategically categorize words into groups, in which one word is not related to the others. Word family organizations work well as do section headings within informational or explanatory texts. *VMCs* or premade laminated words on index cards work very well for this activity and would allow you to address the needs of all learners.

2. Place students in small groups or pairs, if desired. Students could also work alone.

3. Within their groups or independently, have students discuss word meanings and determine which word in each category does not fit.

4. Tell students to create a rejected word list or pull *VMCs* or laminated words aside for a new unknown grouping. As an additional explanatory step, you can require students to write down their rationale for eliminating particular words from the group. This would allow you to gauge and assess student word learning.

5. Students then create a family name or label for the remaining words in the word group. Students may also write an explanation for the label in the form of a word group definition.

6. Direct students to determine if any of the eliminated words belong in an established word family grouping. If so, students then add the previously eliminated word to the word family group list. If words do not fit, then students create a family name for a new category of words.

Example: Complete Word Sort and Verify Method

Court Words	Early Religious Settlers	Local Government	Campaign Words
litigation	~~political parties~~	redistricting	voting
~~voting~~	Puritans	referendum	political parties
plaintiff	Pilgrims	~~platform~~	platform
precedent	Quakers	zoning	
jurisdiction	Moravians	urban renewal	

SORT AND VERIFY

Name ____ Date ____________________

Directions:

1. Sort the words into word family groups.

2. Complete the assigned reading. As you read, verify that you have placed each word in the correct word family by placing a check mark in front of it.

3. If the word is incorrectly placed, move it to the correct column.

4. If you do not find the word in the reading, place a question mark in front of it.

5. Use the last column for words you do not understand.

			Unknown

Word Sort and Verify Words in Context Strategy

To implement the *Sort and Verify Words in Context* strategy, follow these steps:

1. Pre-select the vocabulary words for a specific passage.

2. Give students a chart reflecting how many word families to look for in the reading.

3. Have students begin reading. Direct them to sort words into word family groups as they read. During the sorting, they can label word families as an extension of this step.

4. After reading, students should verify each word as being in the correct word family by placing a check mark in front of the word.

5. If the word is incorrectly placed, students should move the word to the correct column.

6. If students do not find the word in the reading, they should place a question mark in front of it.

7. Include a family labeled "Unknown" to allow students to sort words with which they are unfamiliar and are unable to decipher meaning from the text.

Example: Sort and Verify Words in Context

Word List:

Cultural diffusion, culture, ethnic group, cultural hearth, cultural region, Mesopotamia, Indus River Valley, Mesoamerica, West Africa, Ganges River Valley, Wei-Huang Valley, Ganges River Valley, Nile River Valley, literature, arts, music, food, linguistics, language, laws, mores, customs, beliefs, knowledge, global society, global citizen, globalization

Cultural Hearths/ Regions		Cultural Diffusion		Culture		Unknown	
√	Nile River Valley	√	culture	√	ethnic group	?	mores
√	Indus River Valley	√	diffusion	√	literature	?	linguistics
√	Wei-Huang Valley	√	direct diffusion	√	arts	?	global citizen
√	Ganges River Valley	√	indirect diffusion	√	music	?	global society
√	Mesopotamia	√	forced diffusion	√	food		
√	Mesoamerica	√	diffusion	√	beliefs		
√	West Africa	√	globalization	√	language		
				√	laws		
				√	customs		
				√	knowledge		

SORT AND VERIFY WORDS IN CONTEXT

Name ____   Date _______________________

Directions:

1. Take the given word list and sort the words into word family groups as you read the text.

2. After reading verify that you have placed each word in the correct word family by placing a check mark in front of it.

3. If the word is incorrectly placed, move it to the correct column.

4. If you do not find the word in the reading, place a question mark in front of it.

5. Use the last column for words you do not understand.

						Unknown	

◎ Instructional Routine 1: Summary

This first Instructional Routine, *Grouping and Organizing*, provides early and repeated exposures to words. These interventions occur at the beginning and throughout a unit of study. Most are effective tools to use when students are first introduced to new academic vocabulary. The various activities presented in this chapter serve as initial assessments of students' background knowledge and word learning. *Grouping and Organizing* builds students' inductive thinking skills and relational understanding. *Grouping* words helps students build a solid foundation of social studies word awareness. This knowledge base will support student comprehension as they read, encounter new words, and add to word groups. *Organizing* develops students' knowledge of words and concepts through interactions with word meanings. Combined, these strategies help students hone their vocabulary skills in: a) identifying word part patterns, b) sorting word lists into categories and labels, c) connecting words to concepts and topics, and d) relating word groups and word organization to reading. The intervention activities presented in this section promote generative word learning and support cumulative vocabulary knowledge that is further developed in the next four Instructional Routines.

INSTRUCTIONAL ROUTINE 2: MAPPING AND VISUALIZING

Applications

1. Relational mapping and word organizers

2. Visualization strategies

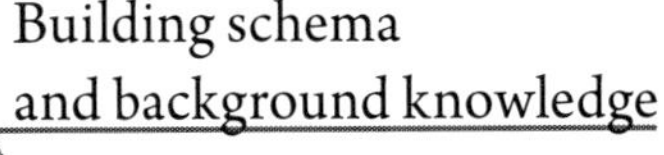

Visual learning is a 21st Century skill and a byproduct of growing up in a ubiquitous technological society. It seems natural that educational environments should harness the power of imagery to support vocabulary development. Mapping is an instructional routine that embraces this potential by providing visual representations of words. The graphic strategies presented could be used for mapping an entire unit's words, mapping groups of words, or mapping individual words. The central focus of this instructional routine is word learning through connections. The connections among words are graphically illustrated by lines and represented with visual clues.

Visual organizers are common ways of mapping words. However, the possibilities for graphic organizers are endless, and trying to choose an organizer to use can be daunting. One way of selecting an organizer is to match the organizer to the structure of the text. This provides students with a visual representation of text structure and helps them understand what is important in the text. Social studies textbooks and documents are usually structured in one of six main formats. Fictional text is most often organized in a narrative format and contains characters, setting, problem, and resolution elements. Nonfiction texts are typically organized in one of the other five text structures: descriptive, cause/effect, sequential, problem/solution, and compare/contrast.

Visual organizers are not the only way to visually represent words and concepts. Other visualizing strategies help support student word learning by visually linking words, word meanings, and words to concepts. In the following activities, *Word Wall* maps are used to literally connect concept, words, and geographical location. While you may choose to show students completed visuals before they read, you can also use all of the visual representations during and after students read. By leaving out some of the words in an organizer or in a map, you can create a reading guide to help students focus on particular sections of text. You can use blank or nearly blank maps or organizers to assess students' understandings at the end of a chapter or unit.

As students map and visualize words, ask these vocabulary comprehension questions to focus student word learning:

1. What does this look like?

2. What is the relationship between these words and/or groups?

3. What is the order represented?

4. What is the sequence?

5. What location is connected to these words?

Application 1: Word Organizers and Relational Mapping

Word organizers and relational mapping are applications of semantic maps, advanced organizers, and graphic organizers. These are powerful tools for reinforcing countless attributes of words and content concepts. They also provide visual representations of word family associations and graphically-oriented concept connections. All of the organizers can be categorized into two formats: list and relational organizers. List organizers, such as *Word Charts* or the *Four Square Matrix,* show the facts or elements of the text but do not indicate a relationship. They simply summarize the information in an easy-to-access way. Relational organizers indicate some type of relationship—for example, common elements, contrasting, overlapping, time-movement, sequence, cause/effect, cyclical, problem/solution, and so on.

Illustrations and templates are presented for each word organizer to visually demonstrate the activity. These are important tools for students to use to build their relational thinking skills. Templates are provided for more complex strategies when specific steps must be replicated with and/or by students. Illustrations are simpler applications and can be modified for each focus word. The illustrations provided can be recreated using drawing tools in any word processing software. There are more sophisticated Web tools that are helpful in creating word organizers. For example, Inspiration© Software Inc. is a very useful diagram creation software designed for educators (http://www.inspiration.com/). This is an education and learner-friendly resource that will allow you and your students to create word organizers and relational mapping tools that will fit any word or concept. The Microsoft Office equivalent is Visio©; although, this software seems more business oriented. A free Web 2.0 tool that you will find useful is *Bubbl.us* (https://bubbl.us). This site offers both you and students the ability to create list or relational organizers for words, word families, and concepts.

Word Organizers

Word Charts

The *Word Chart* is used to examine features of a particular concept or word. *Word Charts* can show synonyms, common attributes, analogies, or examples. Word charts demonstrate cause/effect and problem/solution text structures. They can be informational organizers, such as an *I-Chart.*

Cause/Effect Word Chart:

Cause and effect is a common text structure for social studies text. The *Cause/Effect Word Chart* helps students identify a particular event, such as the passage of legislation or a pivotal point in history, and expand the event to include cause or causes and effects. It can be used to introduce a new word or as a review and assessment of student word learning.

Initial use of the *Cause/Effect Word Chart* will begin with you identifying the event using the following template. Display the template to the whole class. Students can draw their own version or you can share copies with them. You will then direct students to identify the causes and effects from alternate sources. For example, you may decide to show an initial video clip that summarizes the causes for the event. You may then ask the students to read the textbook and find the effects or outcomes of the specified event. At the end of the unit or as a summative assessment, you can give students a blank chart to evaluate student word learning. The chart at this point serves as a memory tool in helping students recall important information related to the event.

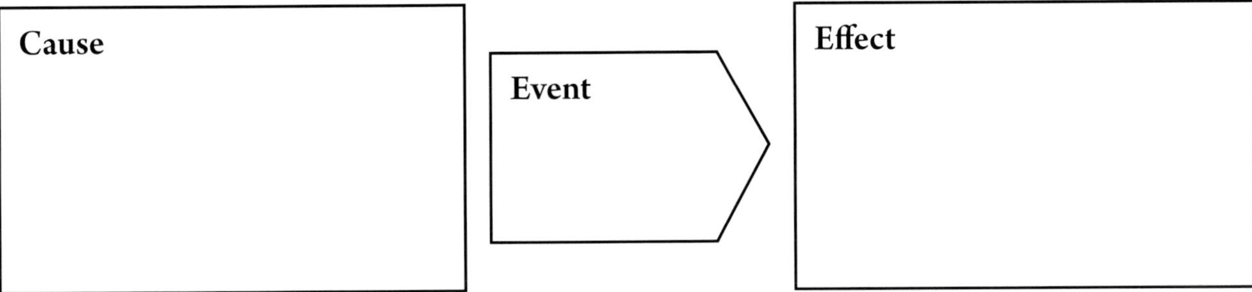

I-Chart (Information Chart):

The *I-Chart* is a tool that helps students select and then summarize information across sources. It is an advanced organizer that scaffolds students reading comprehension and sourcing of information. The *I-Chart* is also applicable for guiding student research. The *I-Chart* is most effective when used to explore in more detail a topic or concept. This Word Chart can be applied at any point in an instructional unit. Students do not have to be familiar with the focus prior to the activity.

Your use of this *Word Chart* begins with defining a focus (indicated by the three blank lines in the sample chart) for student reading. For example, a specific individual, experience, political view, societal issue/problem, or geographic influence may serve as the I-Chart focus. Next you will offer students a variety of sources that relate to the focus. These sources might include photographs, Web sites, excerpts of textbooks, primary documents, video clips, and maps. The students complete the *Before Reading* section of the *I-Chart*. After the students read, they return to the I-Chart and complete the *After Reading* columns. Students conclude by looking across the sources and writing a summary statement that captures their learning about the initial focus.

I-CHART

Name _______________________________________   Date _______________________

Directions:

1. Choose three to five sources that will give you *the best* understanding of _________________ and explain why. List these in the Source column.

2. Under "Before Reading: What information/evidence will this source give?" justify your selection by describing what type of information you expect to find.

3. After you read the source, complete the last two columns, labeled "After Reading."

4. Once you have completed the I-Chart, look across each of your sources and write a summary statement that describes your learning about the focus.

Source:	*Before Reading:* What information/evidence will this source give you?	*After Reading:* What information did you find about _______________?	*After Reading:* What inferences about _____________ might you make from this evidence?

In a meaningful way, describe what you have learned about ___________________________________.

____

____

Four-Square Matrix

With the *Four-Square Matrix,* students can show multiple features of a word or concept, such as a visual depiction, a quote from the text, or synonyms and antonyms of the word. The matrix is also appropriate to show main points of descriptive and narrative text.

To create a matrix, students divide a 3" x 5" note card into four boxes (see below) and then write a vocabulary word at the top of the card. In the first box students write a definition of the word. In the second box they write the sentence or sentences in which the word is used. In the third box they place antonyms and synonyms for the word—or what the word is and isn't. In the fourth box they can draw a visual representation of the word.

The matrix can be adapted to fit a narrative text by using one box to list characters, one for setting, one for the text's problem, and one for the problem's resolution. To adapt the matrix to a descriptive text, ask students to show three main points of the text in the first three boxes and use the final box to write either a personal reflection or a summary of the text.

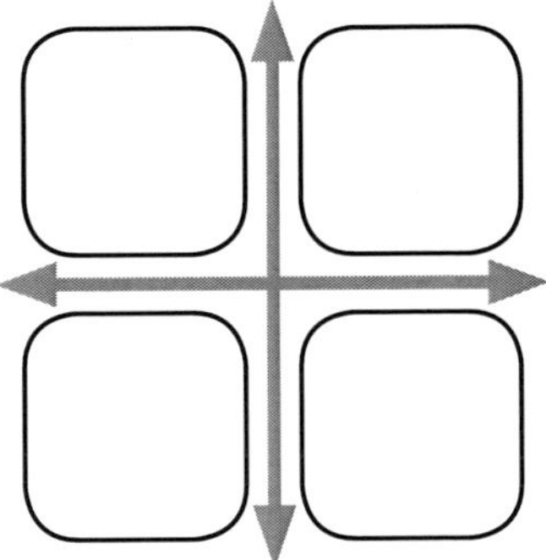

A variation of the *Four-Square Matrix* is to use a foldable matrix in which students create flaps for each square. Students fold a piece of 8" x 10" paper in half and then fold each halve equally toward the center of the paper. A student example follows.

Example: Four-Square Matrix

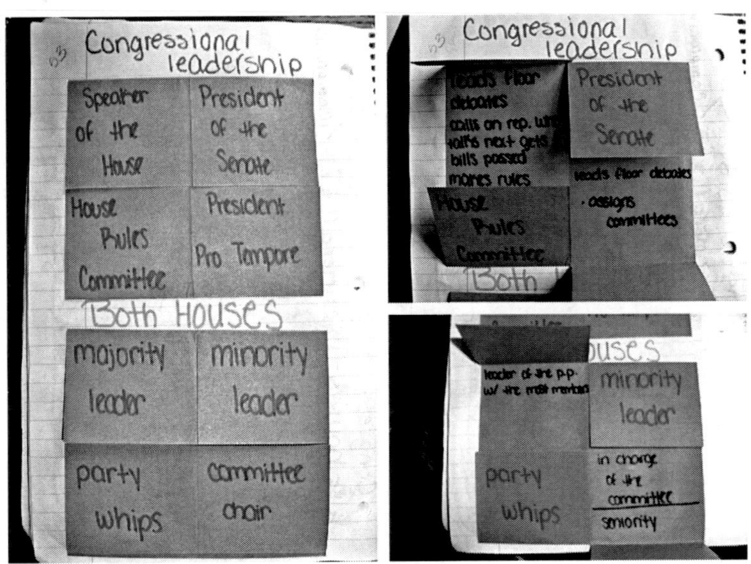

Four-Square Matrix Foldable Template

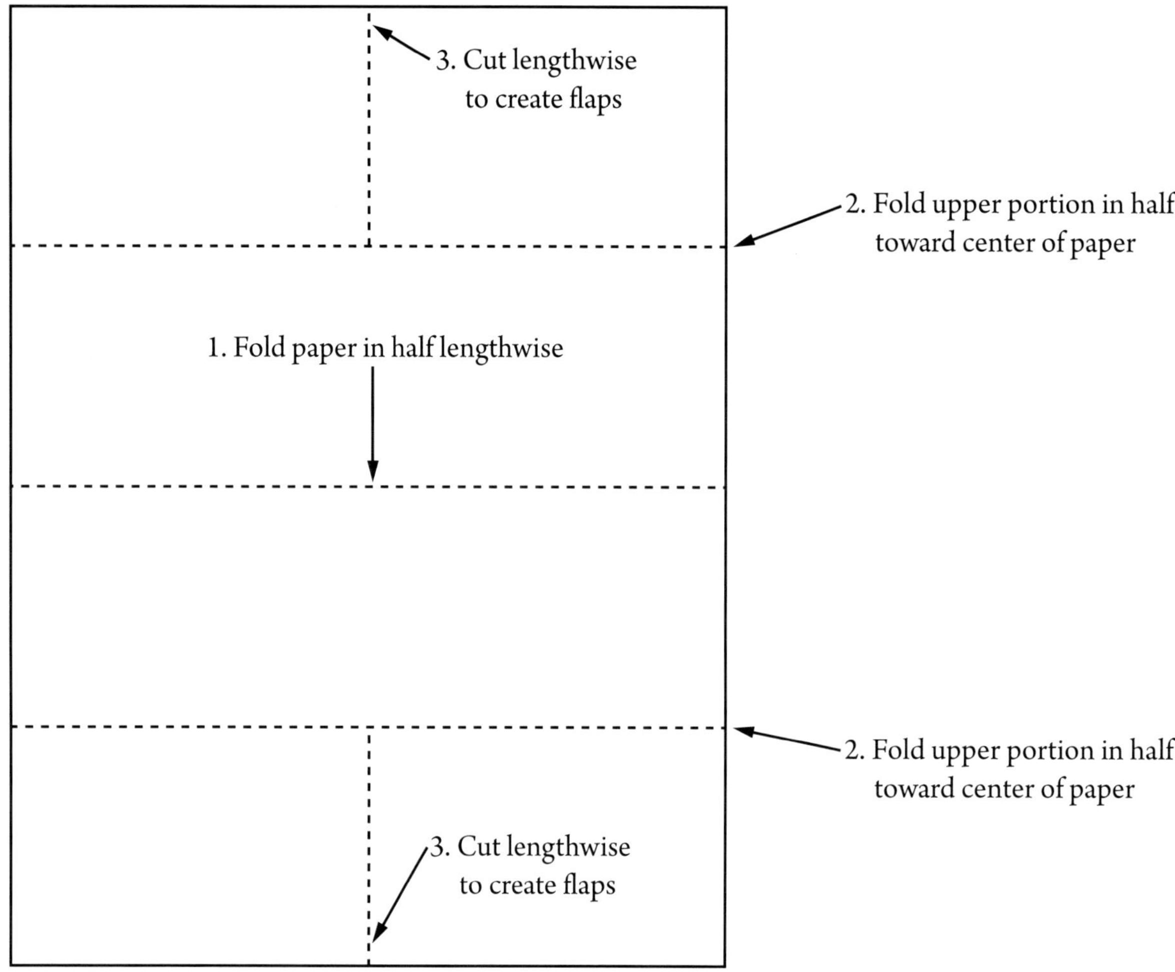

Relational Organizers

Bubble Maps

You can use *Bubble Maps* to assess students' prior knowledge of a concept, or students can use them to gather facts about a major concept. Students begin by writing the target word in the center circle and related vocabulary or important associated concepts at each spoke. Students might also list a cause in the center and its resulting effects in surrounding circles. This is a good strategy for descriptive and informational texts. It is helpful to use this activity when you first introduce students to a word or concept. The strategy is also applicable for student use as a during-reading activity. In this sense, students use the *Bubble Map* to connect particular ideas to the overall concept of a reading or lesson. You can extend this activity by asking that students create a second tier of bubbles and place related terms that define word associations.

Bubble Maps Word Chart

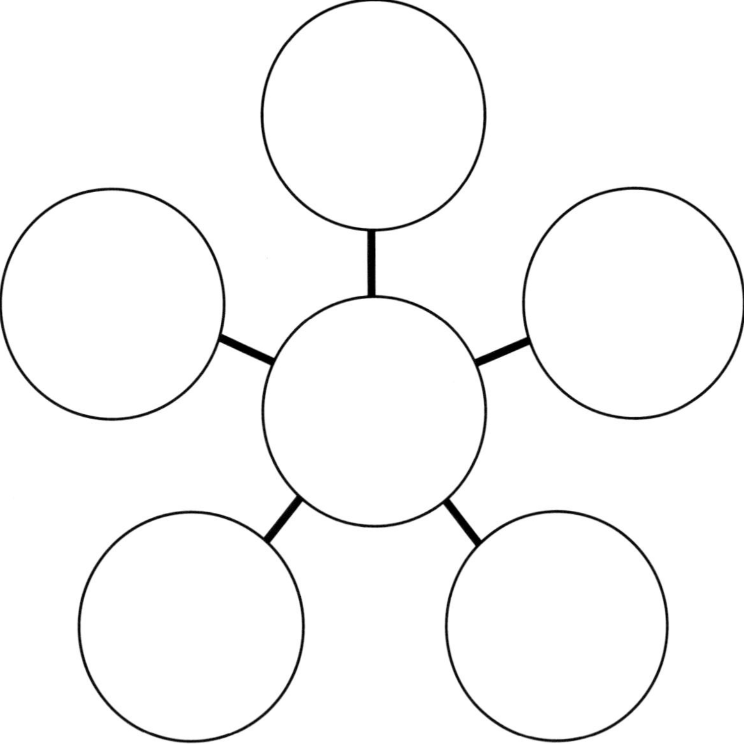

Bubble Maps Cause/Effect Chart

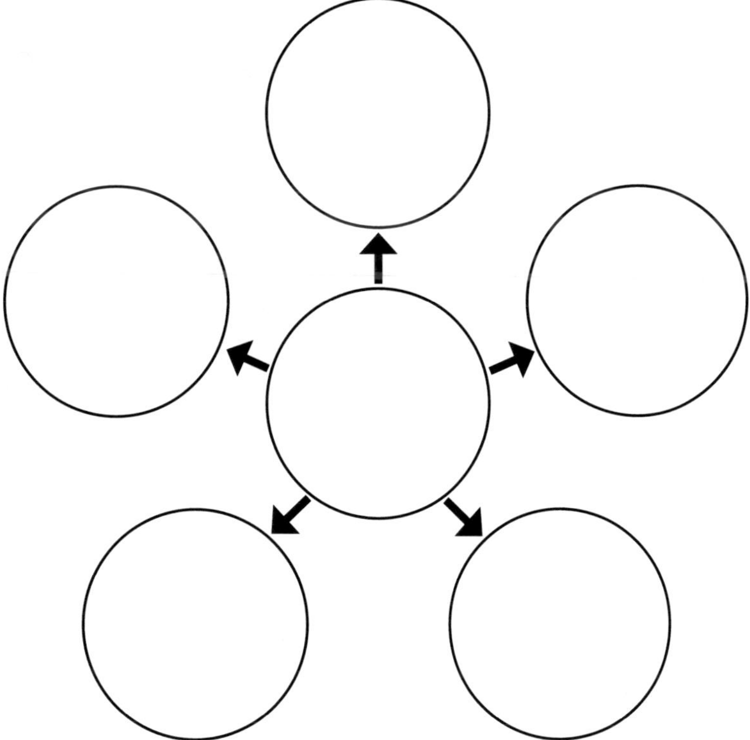

Tree Maps

Tree Maps visually present sequential or categorical information. They also promote relational word learning. Use *Tree Maps* to have students chart word families and their relationships to the each other and a broader concept. Additionally, *Tree Maps* are appropriate for cause/effect and problem/solution text formats. When complete, these organizers show the relationship between a cause and multiple effects or a problem and multiple solutions.

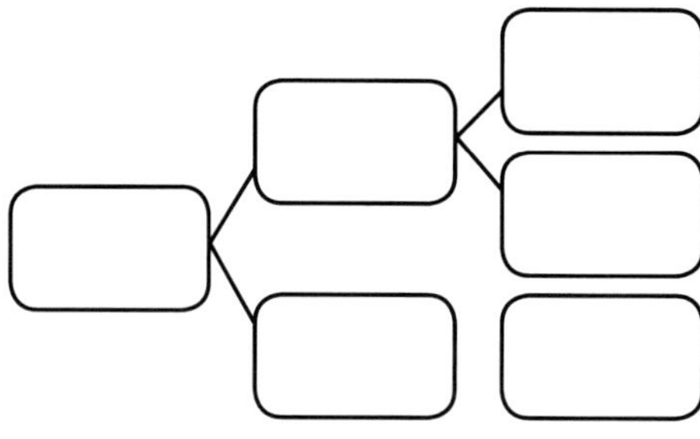

Linear Arrays

Linear Arrays are appropriate to use for target words that present either a chronological concept (such as a historical era), or degrees of something (such as government hierarchy). Because these organizers show the relationship between time and events, they are particularly useful with text that is sequentially organized (such as narratives). *Linear Arrays* can also be used with text organized in a problem/solution format.

Cyclical Maps

Cyclical Maps are appropriate for showing words as they relate to broader concepts or to show how a single word relates to an overall concept. It is a particularly useful tool with text that describes any kind of cycle. You can also use *Cyclical Maps* to show the steps in a problem/solution or cause/effect text.

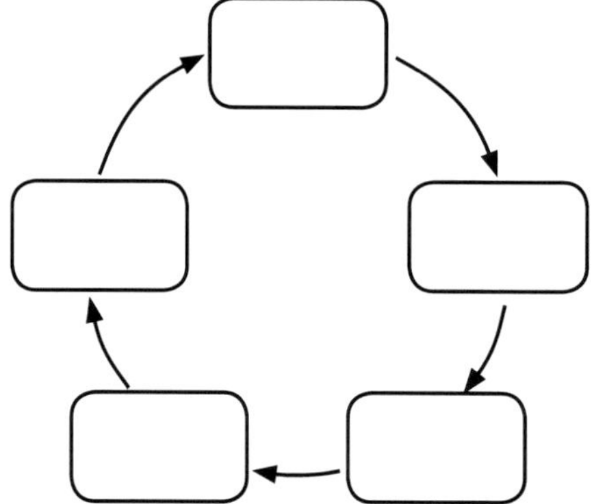

Example: Cyclical Map

Use *Cyclical Map* to demonstrate the relationship among the three branches of government: Judicial, Executive, and Legislative. Include the powers of each branch and limitations of these powers. Be sure to add the checks that each branch performs on the other to branches of government. This concept map should demonstrate the American system of separation of powers and the system of checks and balances.

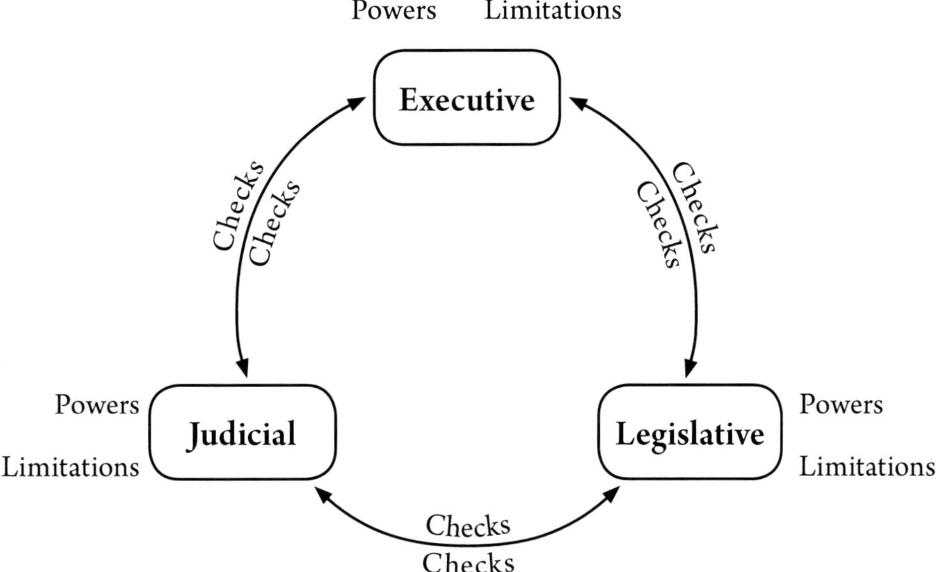

Squares & Roots

Use *Squares & Roots* to develop relational word learning. The application of this word organizer will help students explore word roots and develop their own word meanings. You can use this activity as an extension of *Words Are All Greek to Me,* but the focus here is on generative word learning and the independent creation of word meanings. You should use this relational organizer to develop student skills in crafting word definitions. It is also an opportunity for multiple word exposures and to promote higher levels of word awareness.

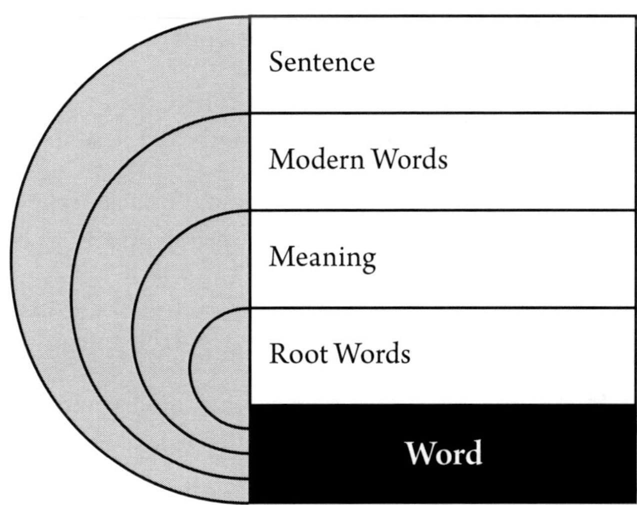

Example: Squares & Roots

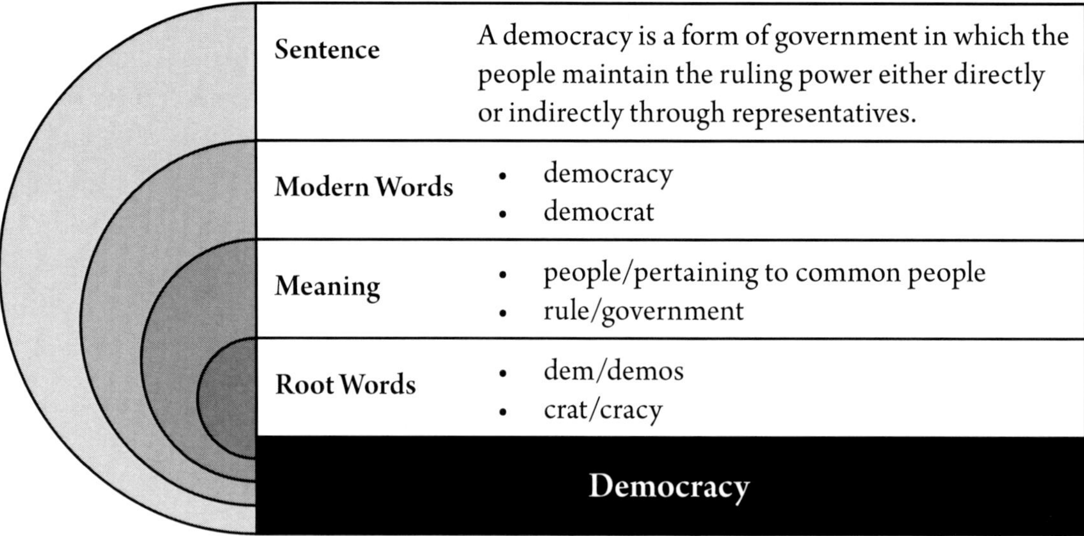

Foldable Squares & Roots

You can use the same components of the *Squares and Roots* strategy in a more manipulative format. A foldable template is provided that will allow you and students to create an interactive version of Squares and Roots. To use this activity, follow these steps:

1. Copy a template of the foldable onto a single piece of paper.

2. Have students make the foldable by folding the paper along the dotted lines. Folds should look like the following picture.

3. Direct students to identify the word root and modern forms of the word using an online source (Source to use could include: http://www.etymonline.com, http://www.merriam-webster.com/dictionary/etymology, http://www.dictionary.net/, or http://www.webster-dictionary.net/). Students will write the root word and modern forms of the word on the appropriate flap.

4. Have students write their own definition for the word on the corresponding flap.

5. Using a text, students add a sentence from their course reading in which the word is used. Students should include the page number and source of the sentence.

6. Tell students to draw an illustration of the word on the back of the foldable. Students can use cut out pictures from magazines, newspapers, or print clip art or pictures from the Internet. Students can also create images using drawing tools.

7. Have students write the word on the inside of the foldable in large print.

8. You can modify the template to support the needs of all learners. Some changes could include having students identify other social studies connections to the word meaning, using analogies, or creating synonyms for words.

Example: Acculturation Foldable Squares and Roots

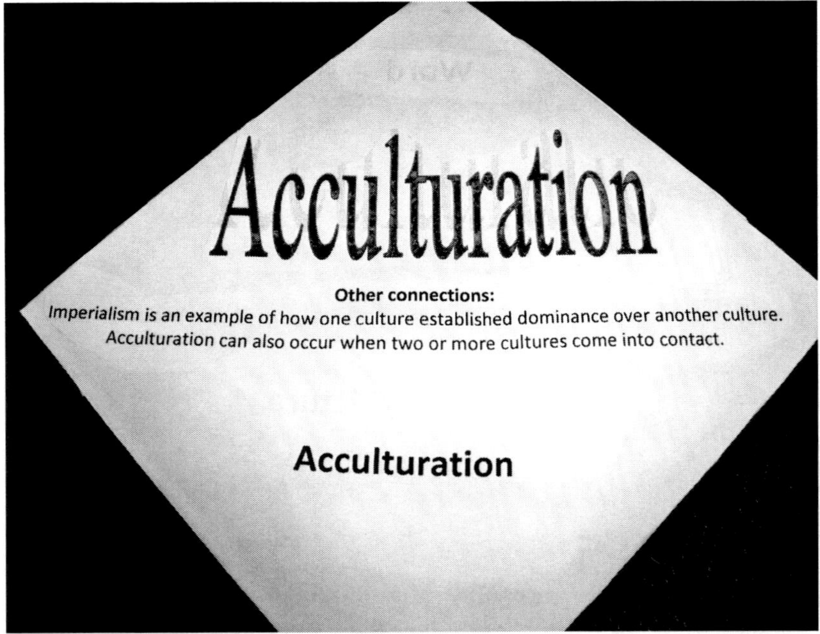

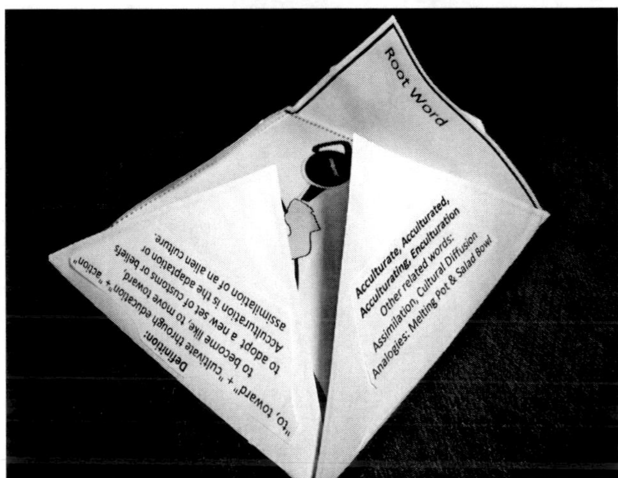

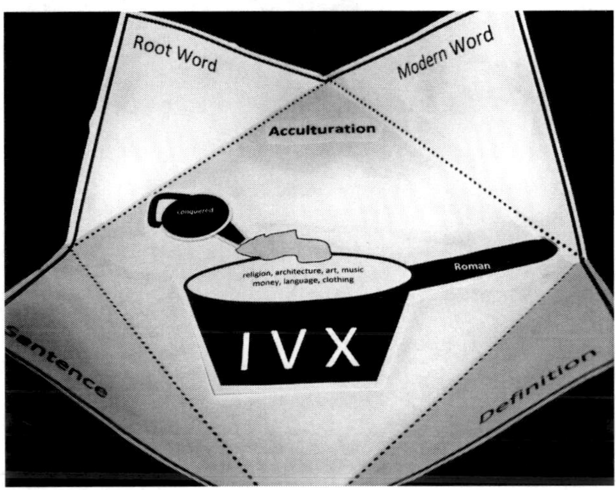

Contents of Acculturation Squares and Roots Foldable

Acculturation

Root Word: ad +culture + ation
prefix =ad   meaning = to or toward; in relation to
root word = culture   to cultivate (till or work) the land
collective set of customs or beliefs (modern meaning)
suffix = ation   makes the noun an action; implies change

Definition: "to, toward" + "cultivate through education"+ "action" / to become like, to move toward, to adopt a new set of customs or beliefs
Acculturation is the adaptation or assimilation of an alien culture.

Sentence: As the Roman Empire expanded, the process of acculturation was used to teach conquered people Roman values, Roman architecture, and the Roman way of life.

Modern Words: Acculturate, Acculturated, Acculturating, Enculturation
Synonyms: Assimilation, Cultural Diffusion
Analogies: Melting Pot & Salad Bowl

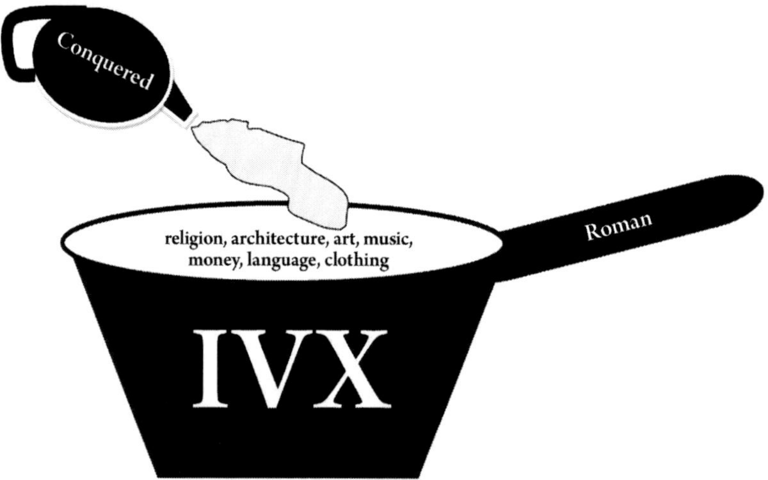

Other connections: Imperialism is an example of how one culture established dominance over another culture. Acculturation can also occur when two or more cultures come into contact.

Squares and Roots Foldable Template

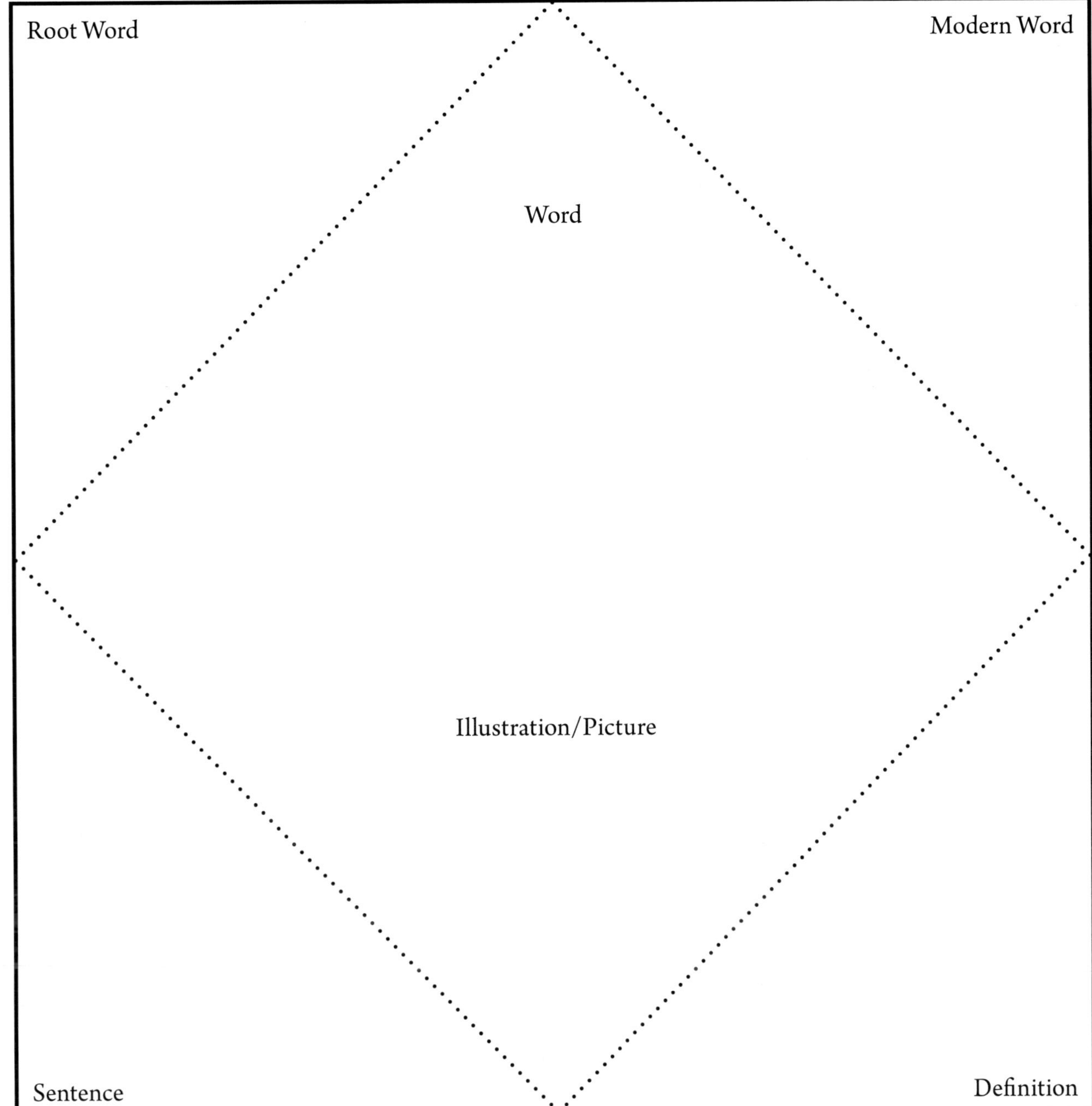

◉ Application 2: Visualization Strategies

Word Walls and Word Maps

Word Wall

Word Wall is a strategy that students can use independently to build and support their vocabulary development in any social studies course. You can have students use *Word Wall* as an initial exposure to words or as a reading comprehension strategy. *Word Wall* is also a great vocabulary review tool. There are many variations for *Word Wall* applications. Some are outlined under differentiated processes, reviewing word walls and word wall riddles. To implement this strategy, follow these steps:

1. Prepare a *Word Wall* with the target vocabulary for the current unit of study.

2. As students encounter the target vocabulary within the class lectures, notes, or reading, have them record the words and accompanying definitions in the *Word Wall* template.

3. Students may add additional words from their reading. An option is to challenge students to add five to ten new words from each reading assignment.

4. Distribute one new *Word Wall* list at the beginning of each unit. Ask students to keep the *Word Wall* templates in a three-ring binder for each unit to give them access to words from previous units. This will encourage students to make connections across units, as well as to review for summative assessments.

Differentiated Process:

-   Have ELL students translate any words into their native languages.

-   Have students look up words and write "hints" next to each target word.

-   When possible, maintain a large *Word Wall* in the classroom for all to see.

-   Students can add new words to the class *Word Wall* as they encounter new words in their reading.

-   As a daily review, ask students to verbally define a selection of words either individually or collectively.

-   At various points in the unit, ask students to sort all of the words from their *Word Walls*. Re-sorting words that they have already sorted while adding new words can provide students with valuable review as well as help them see new ways of sorting previous words.

-   If using *Word Walls* before reading, have students create questions that they predict will be answered in the text.

Reviewing Word Walls: Use *Word Walls* for quick vocabulary review. Place students in small teams. Ask them to consult their completed *Word Wall* templates to answer a variety of questions, such as:

- Which word means…?

- Which word(s) have a root word that means…?

- What is the relationship between word X and word Y?

- What landform describes…?

- Who was president when X occurred?

Award teams points for correct answers. Keep a running score to make the learning process a competitive game.

Reviewing Word Wall Riddles: Ask students to solve riddles using the words on the *Word Wall.* For example, He wasn't king because he said no, but still he helped a new nation to grow. Who was he? (George Washington). Students can then be challenged to make up riddles for opposing teams.

WORD WALL

Name _________________________________   Date _______________________

Unit Vocabulary Words:

A	B	C	D
E	F	G	H
I	J	K	L
M	N	O	P
Q	R	S	T
U	V	W	X, Y, Z

ABC Graffiti

ABC Graffiti is a modified application of *Word Wall*. This strategy is a post-reading activity to help review words and concepts. It brings together both A–Z word strategies with graffiti (writing on walls). However, graffiti is not used in the literal sense but as a way to move portable A–Z word walls among student groups. To implement this strategy, follow these steps:

1. Organize students into four groups. Have students brainstorm concepts from an assigned reading that begin with the letters of the alphabet. Ideas can be either a single word or a phrase. At this point, do not allow students to use the text. You are trying to help students remember what they read. Give groups approximately 5 minutes to accomplish the task.

2. Collect ABC Graffiti sheets from each group and distribute them to another group. Once papers are distributed, have each group continue the brainstorming process on another group's ABC Graffiti sheet. Give groups approximately 5 minutes to accomplish the task. Repeat the process in this step again with the third group.

3. Collect ABC Graffiti sheets from each group and distribute them to the fourth group. The fourth group should write a summary paragraph that integrates the concepts in an organized manner. Give groups approximately 15 minutes to accomplish the task.

4. Collect ABC Graffiti sheets from each group and distribute paper to the original group. Groups should synthesize the summary paragraph and write a topic sentence that describes the meaning of the concepts identified. Give groups approximately 10–15 minutes to accomplish the task.

5. You can conclude with a brief discussion to highlight important concepts from the text. You may also require students to write individually about the text. The writing prompt will be the thesis statement that their group developed.

ABC GRAFFITI

Name _________________________________ Date _____________________

Topic:	
A	**N**
B	**O**
C	**P**
D	**Q**
E	**R**
F	**S**
G	**T**
H	**U**
I	**V**
J	**W**
K	**X**
L	**Y**
M	**Z**

Summary Paragraph:

Topic Sentence:

Word Maps

A *Word Map* illustrates word attributes by geographically associating a list of words with places in the world. This tool brings together geographic thinking and the vocabulary strategy of *Word Wall*. It is a useful strategy for helping students map vocabulary words visually. Generally, a *Word Map* shows a list of words from a single unit of study. You can assign *Word Maps* as an individual activity or you can display one on your classroom wall.

Example: Types of Government Word Map

If you were teaching a unit on types of governments, you might use a *Word Map* like the one below to display terms on a world map.

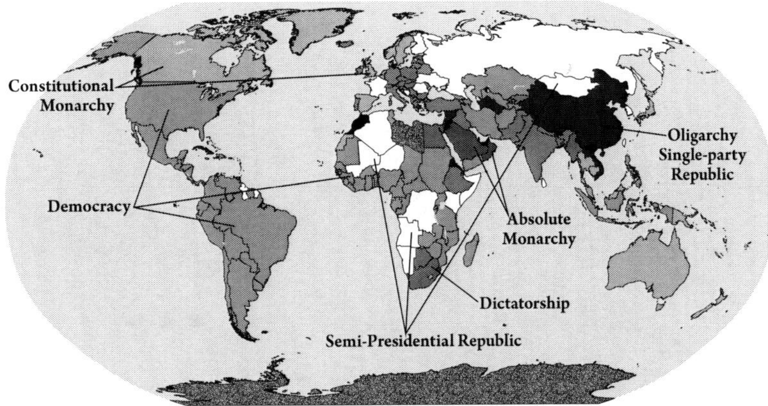

As a modification to this example, you might have students place vocabulary words identifying a form of government next to countries with that particular form of government. You could also place two time-period maps side by side—one from 1811 and one from 2011, for example—so students can compare changes over time using unit vocabulary terms.

Example: World Religions Word Map

This example uses a *Word Map* to help students illustrate vocabulary words associated with a world history unit on world religions. For this unit, students wrote the names of world religions, and terms associated with world religions, on a world map in the area where each religion originated.

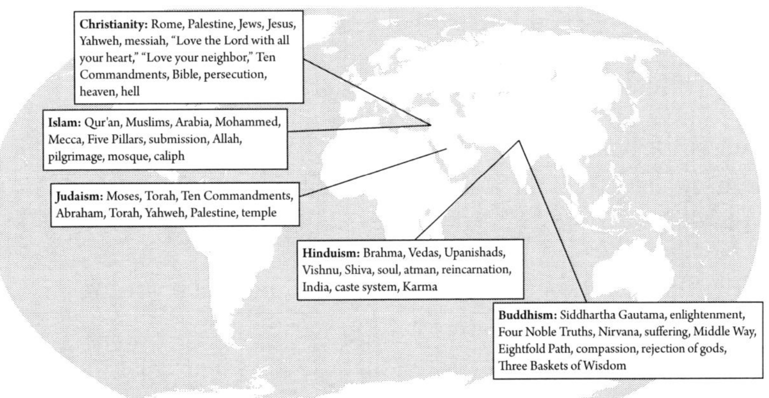

Example: Comparative Advantage Word Map

This student example uses a *Word Map* to illustrate the concept of comparative advantage. Here the student identified resources that are associated with selected regions of the world. The student also included a linked global market between the U.S. and China as an example of one country's comparative advantage over another. The student's inclusion of the term *global interdependence* demonstrates understanding of the connection between natural resources and global markets.

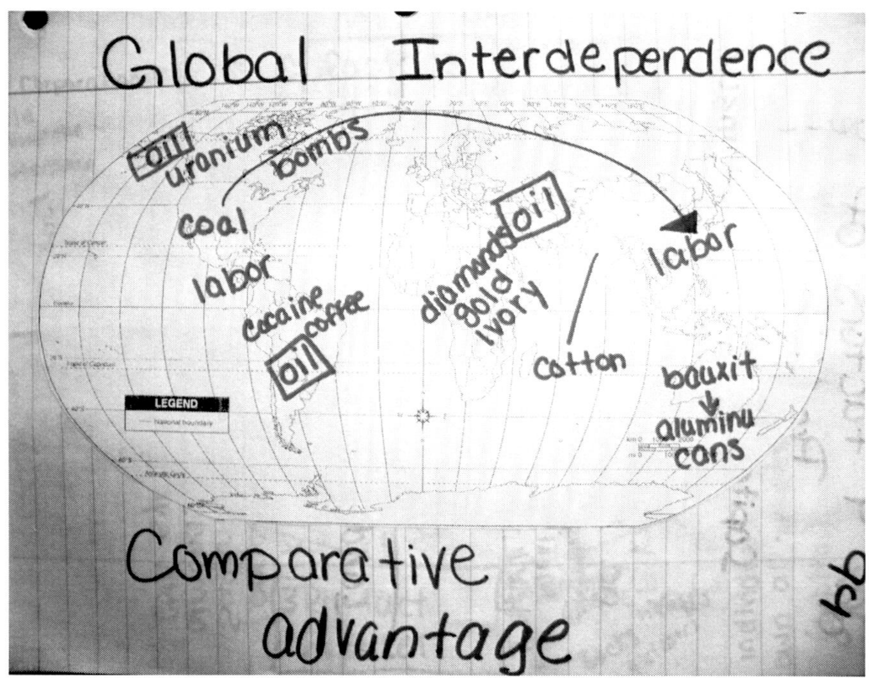

Glogs

Glogster (http://www.glogster.com/) is a social media site where teachers and students create and share Glogs, an online illustrative learning tool. According to *Glogster, Glogs* are "interactive posters loaded with text, graphics, music, videos, and more." This activity of creating a *Glog* is best used when students must conceptualize abstract ideas or major themes. You can use or have students create a *Glog* at any point in a unit: before you start the unit, during instruction, or after students finish the unit. To implement this strategy, follow these steps.

1. Choose words from the concept list that can be illustrated.

2. Brainstorm a visual representation of each word as a whole class.

3. Assign each student to a group of no more than four students. Give each group a single word and a planning sheet. You can also have students work individually and share their ideas in small groups.

4. Students then create a *Glog* at http://edu.glogster.com/. (If you are visiting the site for the first time, you will have to register before getting started.) The *Glog* should include the word, a visual representation of the word, a paragraph that explains the visual, and the excerpt of text where the word is used.

Differentiated Process:

- If you have access to a computer lab, finish the activity with a gallery walk, in which perhaps five students stand at computers to present their *Glogs* to the class, while other students circulate to see the work of their peers.

- Have students delete the word from their *Glogs* and see if students from other groups can guess which word they were assigned.

- You can also have students create a *Glog*-like product in PowerPoint® or as a hard-copy poster.

Example: Harriet Tubman Glog[1]

Example: 1960s Glog[2]

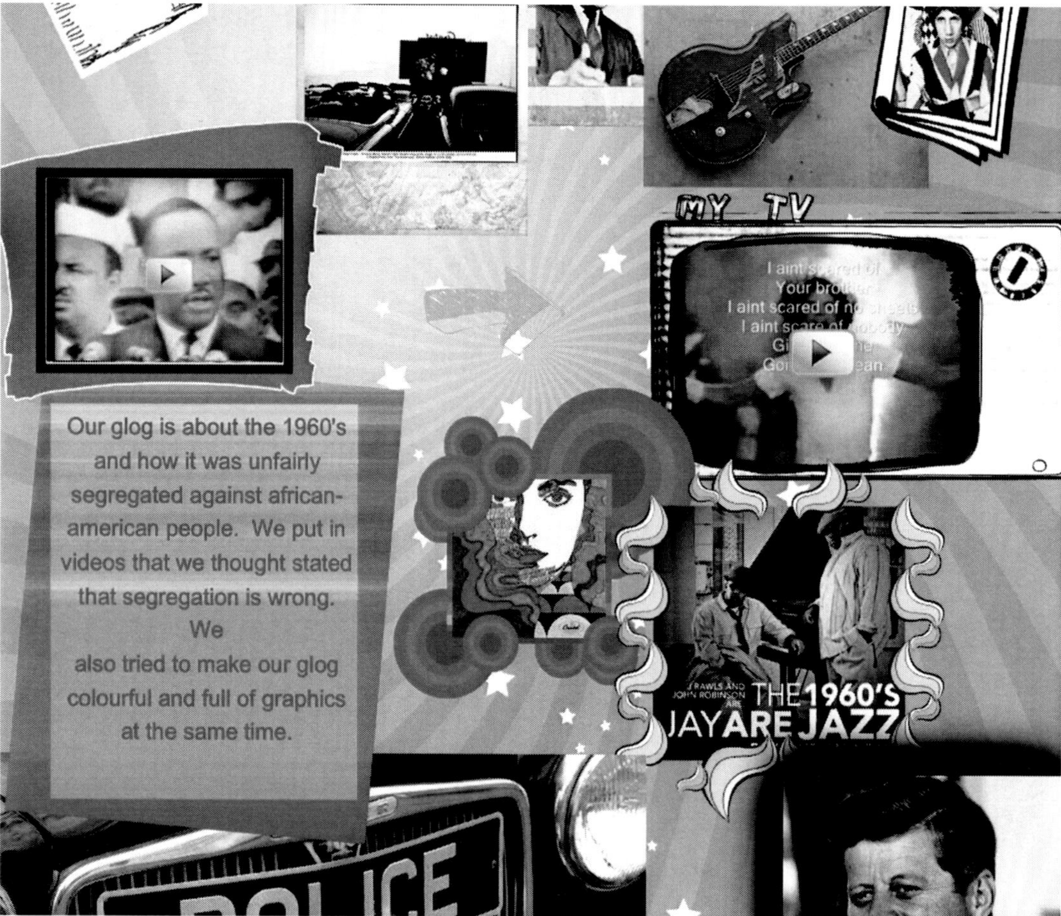

Illustrating Meanings

Because students may be familiar with many of the words in a unit but may not understand those words, it is helpful to take the time to allow students to think about connections among words. *Illustrating Meanings* is a strategy for reinforcing target vocabulary and relational thinking. Using this strategy, students create their own hyperlinks between target vocabulary words and Web material while you assess their developing understandings. You can make this a pre-reading assignment, or you can assign this in class as a during-reading activity. It is best to use this activity after introducing the unit and target words to students. You can assign students individual words or they can choose from a list. You may want to establish some guidelines to ensure accurate word associations are made. These guidelines might include requirements that links should have a reference to the supporting textbook/text or should include a reference to the ruler, country, government, and so on. To implement this strategy, follow these steps:

1. Give each student a passage from the text or an associated work of literature.

2. Underline or supply a list of words that the students will find in the text.

---

2 Source: http://edu.glogster.com. Permission granted for reproduction.

3. Ask students to retype the passage into a Word document, PowerPoint® file, or an online presentation tool, such as *Prezi.com* (http://prezi.com/).

4. For each identified word, students create a hyperlink to an image, Web site, or document that illustrates and supports the identified word.

Example: Illustrating Meanings Document Version

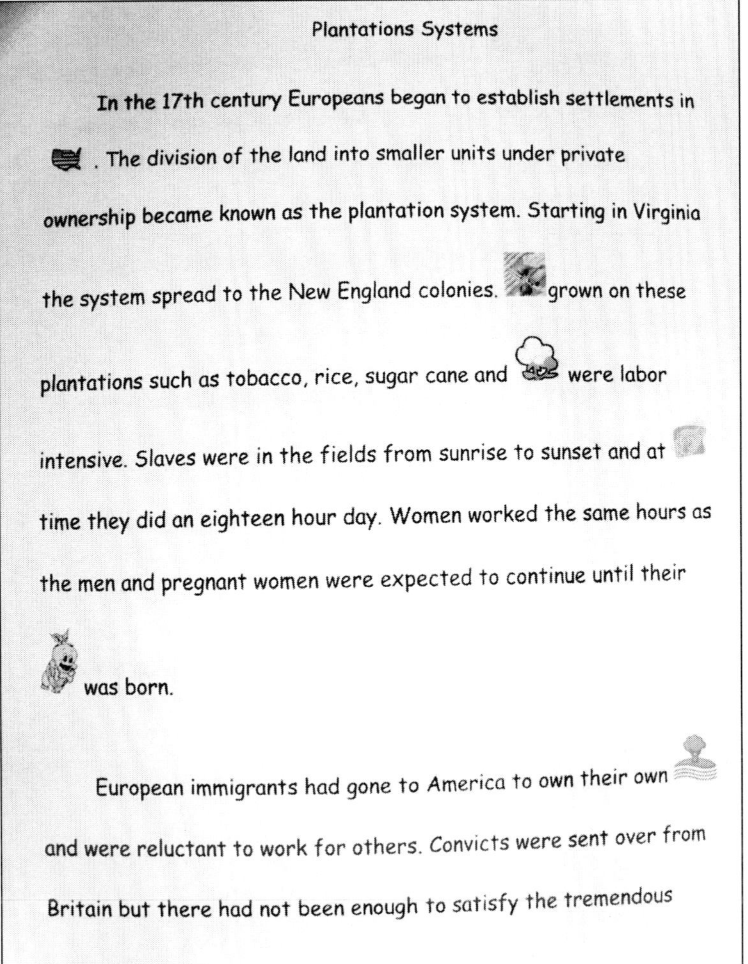

Differentiated Process:

- Have each student write an original passage, using the assigned words and replacing them with hyperlinks. Then have them exchange papers with partners. Each student then tries to identify his or her partner's illustrations.

- Students may choose their own words to illustrate, identifying those that they have difficulty understanding.

- Students may create the hyperlinks in the pattern of a found poem (http://en.wikipedia.org/wiki/Found_poetry).

- Allow students to handwrite the assignment hand-draw the illustrations.

- In a variation of this strategy called *Focused Cloze,* you could copy a passage from the text, inserting blank lines in place of targeted vocabulary words. You can then ask students to insert illustrated meanings and words in the blanks.

Example: Illustrating Meanings with Focused Cloze

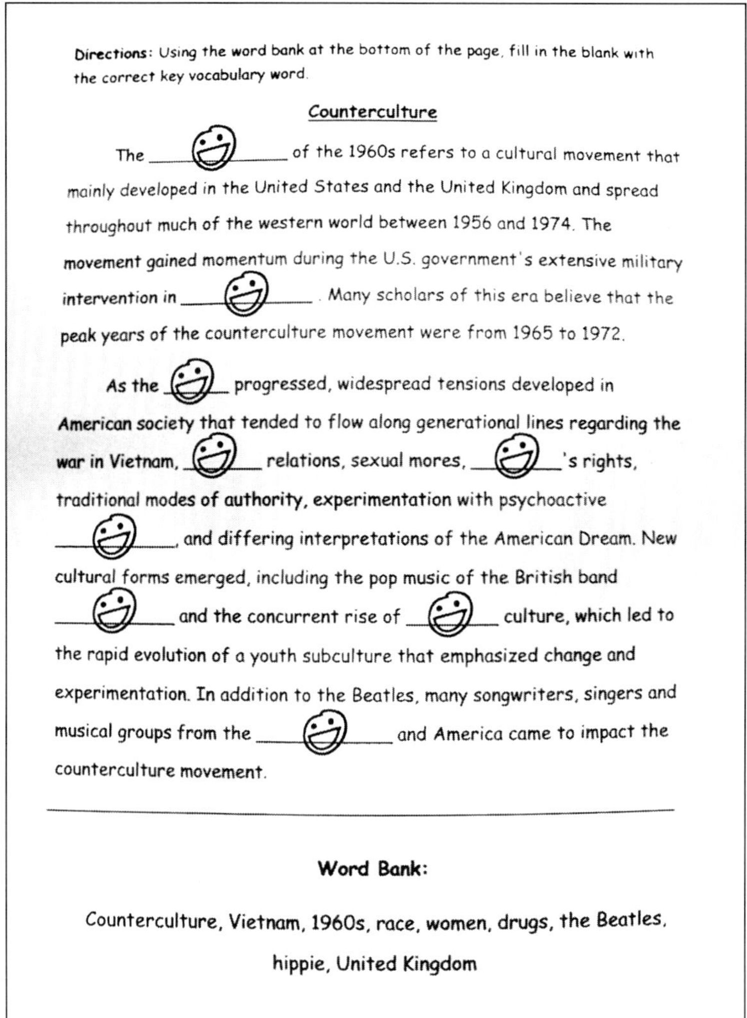

Vocabulary Visualization Web Tools

Students can illustrate word meanings with visual representations that they create with *Web Tools.* Using Web sites, students create visual links to word meanings, allowing them to assess their awareness and develop a deeper understanding of words. You can use this activity as a group project or independent activity. The application of *Web Tools* allows students to engage creatively with the target vocabulary. To implement this strategy, follow these steps.

1. Give each student a list of target words. It is fine to give the same list to all students.

2. Introduce students to one of these *Web Tools:*

   - *Comic Life:* http://www.comiclife.com/

   - *GoAnimate!:* http://www.goanimate.com/

   - Prezi: http://www.prezi.com/

   - *ToonDoo:* http://www.toondoo.com/

3. Following the instructions on these sites, have students create a comic, animation, political cartoon or interactive presentation that illustrates their understanding of each word. Students can also create comic versions of events found in informational texts they are reading. You can ask students to create an entirely new context in which to use the vocabulary.

4. Give students opportunities to share their finished products.

Web Tools

- Comic Life: http://www.plasq.com/education/ Comic Life lets students create their own comics to illustrate a particular word or concept.

- GoAnimate!: http://www.goanimate.com/ GoAnimate! allows students to create their own video and add voice. This makes it possible to animate words and concepts.

- Prezi: http://www.prezi.com/ Prezi enables students to develop interactive visual presentations. This tool allows students to manipulate images, add sound, and use other tools more easily than traditional presentation software (e.g. PowerPoint®).

- ToonDoo: http://www.toondoo.com/ ToonDoo allows students to create their own comic strips and graphic novels. It is also a useful resource for creating political cartoons.

Examples: Web Tools

If you were teaching a unit on types of governments, students might use Web Tools to create a visual illustration like those shown on the following Web sites:

- http://www.metacafe.com/watch/yt-DioQooFIcgE/the_american_form_of_government

- http://www.toondoo.com/Search.toon?searchfield=governments&searchFrom=toon

- http://www.toondoo.com/Search.toon?searchfield=government&searchFrom=toon

- http://goanimate.com/movie/0mIZlO-7MhRA

- http://goanimate.com/movie/0ALkf4u7Fveg

- http://prezi.com/oqibtsfwljpi/types-of-government/

Example: Comic Life

The *Comic Life* (www.comiclife.com) Web site is a good tool for teachers or students to use to create word meanings visually. For example, students could use Comic Life to illustrate colonial life, the impact of colonization, or the outcomes of the Columbian Exchange. The following picture of Columbus' journey is an interpretive example of exploration that is available on Comic Life's Web site under the tab for history (http://plasq.com/education/#history).[3]

---

3 *Columbus.* Work is attributed to Marilee Sarlitto, Kildeer School. Source: http://plasq.com/data/images/comiclife/education/Explorer_comic.jpg

Students could also use Comic Life to illustrate a day in the life of a slave. The following picture of depicts a slave's life and is available on Comic Life's Web site under the tab for history (http://plasq.com/education/#history).[4]

4 *A Day in the Life of a Slave.* Work is attributed to Nicholas S. of Kildeer School. Permission granted for reproduction. Source: http://plasq.com/data/images/comiclife/education/Slave_comic.jpg

Word Art

Word Art further emphasizes the visual representation of words and illustrates meanings that are of particular importance to word learning. You can use this activity to demonstrate a variety of aspects associated with vocabulary comprehension. The method is especially effective as a pre-reading strategy or as a primary source analysis tool. You can also use it to emphasize vocabulary words that are central to the understanding of a document. You can introduce *Word Art* as a visually projected word list. Then have students either individually or collectively define the terms before they begin reading.

An excellent tool for this strategy is *Wordle.net,* a Web site that calculates the frequency of word use in documents. All you have to do is copy and paste a document into the site at http://www.wordle.net and the site generates a visual image based on the number of occurrences of words. To use *Word Art,* follow these steps:

1. Learn more about *Wordle.net* at http://www.wordle.net/faq

2. Break the class into pairs or groups.

3. Choose words from the concept list that can be reinforced through group discussion and word study.

4. Have students experiment with *Wordle.net* and complete the planning sheet (see page 81).

5. Create a Wordle that demonstrates comprehension of one of the following:

   - related terms

   - synonyms

   - antonyms

   - members of the same category (people, historical documents, landforms)

6. *Wordle.net* determines the size of a word based on the number of times that word appears in the document. Have students utilize this feature to demonstrate a hierarchy to the word list (most similar, most different, etc.). Have students write a paragraph explaining their rationale.

Web Tools

Wordle.net: Wordle allows the user to create a word cluster from a source text. Students or teachers enter a text. The Web site shows the most frequently used words in the text as the largest in the word cluster.

Example: Word Art

Reading Selection: "The Meaning of July Fourth for the Negro"
From *The Life and Writings of Frederick Douglass,* Volume II
Pre-Civil War Decade 1850–1860
Philip S. Foner
New York: International Publishers Co., 1950

Example: Word Art Planning Sheet

Word:	
Word in context from the text:	
Word meaning based on glossary, class discussion and/or dictionary:	
Associated word list:	
Words to emphasize:	
Draft of paragraph that explains your approach to creating the Wordle. Why are some words bigger than others? Which words did you choose to include, and why?	

Visual Inventory

Visual Inventory is a strategy for teaching vocabulary using traditional images, such as paintings and photographs, to help students learn words and make connections to a central concept. This strategy promotes inductive thinking by using images as a mnemonic device to promote site word vocabulary learning. The *Visual Inventory* strategy draws from Joyce, Weil, & Calhoun's (2009) Picture Word Inductive Model (PWIM) for early vocabulary learning and has been adapted for use with adolescent social studies learners. You can use *Visual Inventory* as an introduction to a concept or as a review. It is also a very effective pre- or post-assessment of student word learning.

It is a good idea to use art or photographs that are very detailed and provide rich examples of vocabulary needed to understand a concept. For example, John Gast's painting *American Progress* effectively illustrates the concept of Manifest Destiny and such details as the telegraph, Pony Express, competing railroads, Indian Removal, steamboats, light vs. dark, stagecoach, and mining to explain the migration westward and rationale for expansionist thinking of the late 1800s.

To implement this strategy, follow these steps:

1. Select a painting or photograph that contains rich details.

2. Project the image to the whole class.

3. Ask students to identify what they see in the image. Identify for students any word attributes or examples of the overall concept or topic presented in the image.

4. Have students write details on their own sticky notes or on an interactive whiteboard so they are able to highlight the details on the projected image.

5. Discuss student responses to the visual inventory.

6. Provide additional content and contextual information to help students understand the details of the image and the overall concept.

Differentiated Process:

Provide students with the vocabulary words. Have students match the words to the detail in the image. They can do this with premade laminated word cards, such as *VMCs,* or a list of words you have created on the interactive whiteboard that you can display and place over the image by dragging the words.

Visual Inventory Example 1: Smallpox—The Black Death in Action[5]

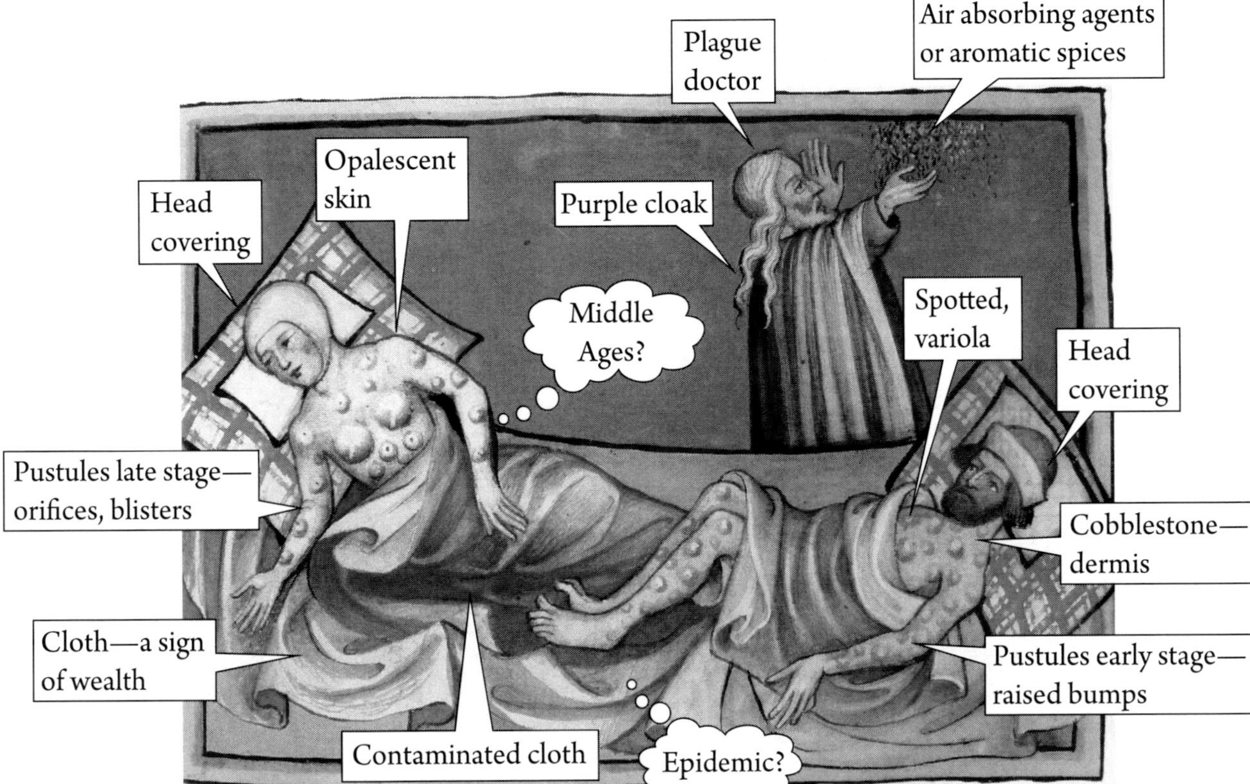

Here are some student observations and responses to the image:

Visual Inventory: woman on bed, man on bed, blood, doctor, clothing, cloth, postulates on bodies, male and female head coverings, some sort of medicine practice

Background: I don't know anything about this picture but my be a long time ago, perhaps Middle Ages.

Connections:

- There are more people dying than alive. This might mean large scale death. Was this an epidemic?

- The sores remind me of cobblestone streets. Are they smallpox? Also, didn't the Black Death have something to do with smallpox?

- These people are all white. Are they European? Didn't the Black Death occur in Europe in the Middle Ages?

- Interpretations: I think this is a picture showing the Black Death because the man and woman on the bed have bodies covered in pustules. They show symptoms and signs of smallpox. I think the purple robed man is a doctor. The purple robe is a sign of wealth or status. He is throwing something into the air. I think what he was doing was a practice for treating smallpox.

---

5 While the teacher in this example states that the Black Death was a smallpox epidemic, the more widely-held belief amongst historians is that the disease that swept across Europe in the 14th century was a form of *Yersinia pestis*, the bacterium responsible for the pneumonic, septicimic, and bubonic plagues.

Questions: Is smallpox an airborne disease? What causes smallpox? What were medical practices (like what the doctor is throwing into the air) during the Black Death?

The teacher used this image to introduce vocabulary words (see following list) that students needed to know in order to read a one page excerpt from "The Demon in the Freezer." This was also an introductory lesson for a unit on how disease impacts society. She followed the visual inventory with a vocabulary word list from the text.

Vocabulary

- Smallpox
- Virus
- Egypt
- Pharaohs
- Parasites
- Affinity
- Eradicated
- Cobblestone street
- Pustules
- Opalescent
- Dermis
- Variola
- WHO: World Health Organization
- Black Death
- Middle Ages
- Orifices
- Epidemic

After reviewing words not that were identified in the image, she asked students to predict the connections that remaining words might have. She provided etymologies of other related, but unfamiliar words, e.g. Variola.

Variola = spotted
derived from the Latin varius (spotted) or varus (pimple)
variola, first used during the 6th century by Bishop Marius of Avenches (Switzerland)
Video resource: http://kidshealth.org/kid/health_problems/infection/smallpox.html

The teacher then shared additional information about smallpox:

- How is it spread? Smallpox is easily spread from person to person through breathing. It is also spread through contact with contaminated clothing or bedding. The virus can live for up to one week on an infected object, like a blanket.

- What are mortality rates? According to the WHO, 30% of unvaccinated people die within a couple of weeks. Throughout history, epidemics of smallpox have wiped out entire populations.

- What are historical examples? Examples include: 1) The decimation of Ethiopian soldiers in Hannibal's Elephant War in Mecca in 568 AD; 2) The Black Death in Europe in the Middle Ages; 3) The impact of European exploration to the New World included significant native population reductions in Caribbean in 1507, Mexico in 1520, Peru in 1524, and Brazil in 1555; 4) Hottentots were destroyed in 1713; 5) In 1620 over 90% of North American population wiped out; 6) In 1738 half of the Cherokee Indian population died.

She concluded the visual inventory with these questions as a pre-reading exercise:

- What are symptoms and stages? What are the origins of smallpox? What is the "Demon in the Freezer?"

To answer these questions, students completed the text reading. The teacher selected an excerpt from Richard Preston's *The Demon in the Freezer* which was published in 2002 as the assigned reading. Students expanded word learning through reading the words in the descriptive text. Students used contextual information to further their understanding of word meanings.

Visual Inventory Example 2: Black Death

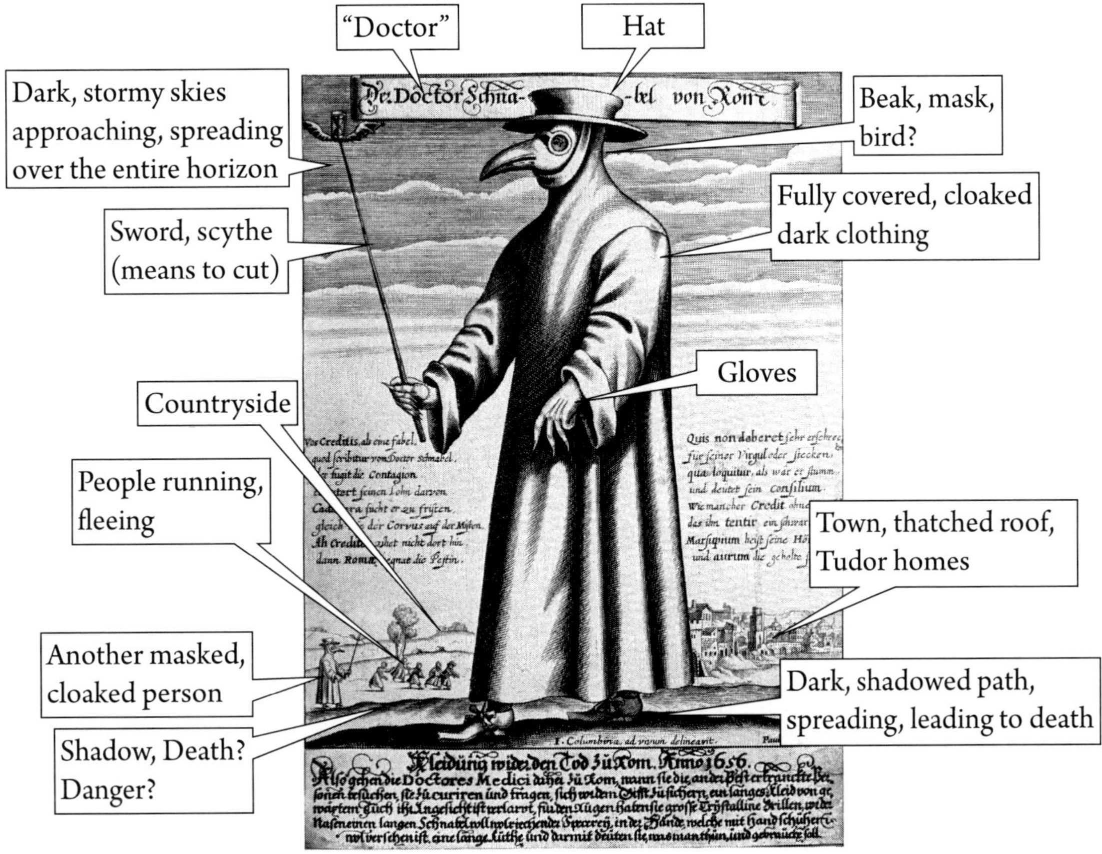

Here are some student observations and responses to the image:

Visual Inventory: masked and cloaked figure, another masked figure in background, people running, town in background, picture in countryside, word doctor in title, dark skies, stormy skies, black path

Background: I don't know anything about this picture.

Connections: It reminds me of Halloween with the masked man. Shadows accompany masked people caring swords? Are they a danger to the town or running people in the picture? Also, didn't the Black Death start in towns? Is that why the people are running into the countryside?

Interpretations: I think this is a picture showing the Black Death because the images foreshadow something dark. I think death is approaching and the masked people represent death. I think that man in the center is a doctor. Another name for a sword is a scythe which means literally to cut. Doctors used bloodletting as a medical treatment for the plague.

Questions: What's up with the mask?

And here is some additional information that the teacher provided:

This picture is indeed about the Black Death. The Black Death was a medieval pandemic that swept through Europe. The Black Death, which wiped out a third of Europe's population in four years, beginning in 1346, was the cause of death for approximately 25 million people. Clues in the painting indicate the location to be in Europe, specifically Great Britain. Architectural design of houses include thatched roofs and Tudor houses indicative of English towns. As an example, you can compare these buildings to houses in Stratford-upon-Avon, a town that has its origins in Saxon culture of medieval England. The plague, a bacterial infection, was found in rodents and discovered to be transferred to humans through fleas. The most dangerous of all rodents to human health were rats. Sanitation and population density were significant factors in the rapid spread of the disease. The central focus of the painting is the plague doctor. The attire of the doctor is most intriguing. Plague doctors cloaked themselves in leathers suits, completely covering their eyes, faces, and extremities. The masks worn included large crystal glasses and a snout. In the "beak" of the mask, doctors placed rags soaked in vinegar or aromatic spices to try and cover the smell of the dead and dying. This was also believed to be a safety precaution from airborne disease along with the fully cloaked attire. They carried a wand or scythe to ward off evils and issue instructions. For a primary source writing describing plague doctors, see: http://jhmas.oxfordjournals.org/content/XX/3/276.extract. This site contains a poem from the 17th Century that provides a satiric description of the plague doctor.

17th Century Poem of a Plague Doctor

> As may be seen on picture here
> In Rome the doctors do appear,
> When to their patients they are called,
> In places by the plague appalled,
> Their hats and cloaks of fashion new,
> Are made of oilcloth, dark of hue,
> Their caps with glasses are designed,
> Their bills with antidotes all lined,
> That foulsome air may do no harm,
> Nor cause the doctor an alarm,
> The staff in hand must serve to show
> Their noble trade where'er they go.[6]

Additional discussions as a follow-up to the reading can lead to examination of Medieval medical practices. For example, bloodletting, stimulants, purgatives, and the use of air absorbing animals (e.g. spiders and toads) were common medical treatments. Symptoms too were interpreted uniquely to the time period. Flushed cheeks were a recognized symptom of early stages of the Black Death. Ailing individuals were taught to exhibit serenity and focus on thoughts of gold or silver that would soothe the mind. Fevers were followed by pustules that erupted into blisters (as presented in the previous visual discovery example) that left the patient (if he/she survived) spotted and scared. Legends develop from historical events such as the Black Death. Scholars trace the origin of the Grim Reaper to ancient times when he was known as Cronus to the Greeks and Saturn to the Romans, but the Grim Reaper as he is depicted today comes directly to us from the Middle Ages and the Black Death.

---

6 http://jhmas.oxfordjournals.org/content/XX/3/276.extract

Follow-up to the use of this image could include similar background content as described in the previous example.

Example: Westward Expansion as American Progress Visual Inventory

American Progress by John Gast, c. 1872

The teacher who showed this image to his class posed the following questions to students as they created word lists:

1. Identify three details you see in the image.

2. What words are associated with these details?

3. Why are these details/words important?

4. What is the relationship between these words?

Students were instructed to write responses to questions 1–3 on post-it notes. Students wrote a response to question 4 in their notes.

To predict the instructional unit topic, the teacher asked students to name the painting. The teacher then instructed students to describe their reasoning for their title as a writing-to-learn exercise. Following student writing, the teacher led a whole class discussion of the painting by having student place their post-its on the projected image. As students identified details in the painting, the teacher asked students to verbally explain what this fact (word) might mean to the overall concept (e.g. painting title). The overarching question that the teacher asked to surmise the discussion was: How would you define Manifest Destiny based on the details in the painting?

◎ Instructional Routine 2: Summary

Mapping and Visualizing techniques allow teachers and students to illustrate words and concepts. The visual component helps clarify relationships between words. Visuals also create representations that can be displayed throughout the unit. Mapping also draws upon imagery tools to visually display relational and geographical thinking. This instructional routine reinforces the vocabulary concepts in ways that students find familiar, memorable, and motivating. It also provides additional layers of word exposures and includes strategies that reinforce text-based word learning. *Mapping and Visualizing* extends initial word learning in the first instructional routine and sets the foundation for more complex generative and relational word learning in the third instructional routine. Since students live in a world full of graphics and are immersed in an ubiquitous technological and global society, it seems natural that social studies classrooms should embrace the power of imagery, technology, and geographic tools to support vocabulary development.

INSTRUCTIONAL ROUTINE 3: COMPARING AND CONTRASTING

Applications

1. Compare and contrast

2. Continuum of meaning

3. Relational analysis

4. What it is and what it is not

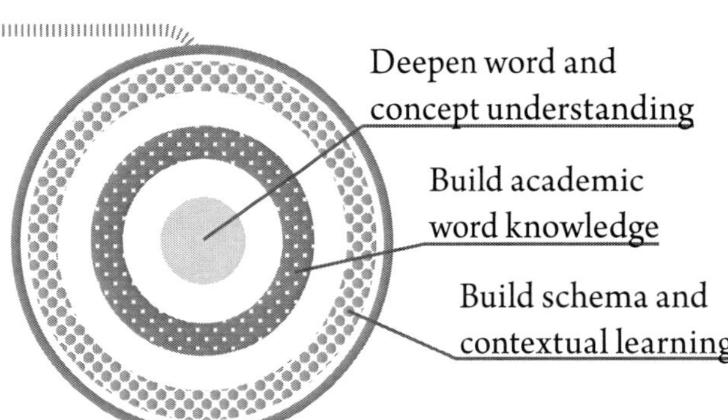

Comparing and Contrasting words helps deepen students' understanding of an overall concept or unit topical focus. While *Grouping and Mapping* words helps students build schema and background knowledge necessary to connect similar words and begin to put them into a general context, *Comparing and Contrasting* allows students to move beyond an initial familiarity with the words they encounter, to unpack word meanings for increased comprehension.

Comparing and Contrasting words also helps students generate understanding about new words. For example, in the *Continuum of Meaning* strategy, students place a specific word on a continuum moving from antonyms to synonyms. This activity helps students gain an understanding of words that might not be in the unit word list and promotes cumulative word learning.

The *Relational Analysis* strategy moves students from comparing single words to comparing concepts. This activity serves to scaffold students' comprehension as they look across ideas and/or texts. For example, in the *Relational Analysis* strategy in the sample World Religions unit, students examine the major tenets of the five main religions in order to compare and contrast these religions. Such comparisons often require students to read a variety of sources. Efficient readers are able to examine multiple sources and synthesize multiple pieces of information. *Relational Analysis* provides the scaffold for students to approach this task.

Through *Comparing and Contrasting*, students develop a more complex knowledge of social studies words. Increased vocabulary knowledge builds content background knowledge and predicts comprehension. Further, as students learn to compare and contrast meanings, they are better prepared to transfer this process to other content and generate their own vocabulary learning.

As students compare and contrast words, ask these vocabulary comprehension questions to focus student word learning:

1. What does this word mean?

2. How did this word acquire this meaning?

3. What associations can be made with this word?

4. How are these words/families of words alike?

5. How are these words/families of words different?

◎ Application 1: Compare and Contrast Organizers

Comparing and Contrast Organizers are applications of semantic maps, advanced organizers, and graphic organizers. These are powerful tools for reinforcing countless attributes of words and content concepts. They also provide visual representations of word family associations and graphically-oriented concept connections. They simply summarize the information in an easy-to-access way.

Useful Web tools introduce in the last chapter are also a good resources for creating *Comparing and Contrast Organizers.* You can use the *Bubbl.us* (https://bubbl.us) Web site to create comparison and contrasting organizers for words, word families, and concepts. Other helpful organizer creator Web tools that can be purchased are: Inspiration® and Visio®.

Venn Diagrams

Use this organizer to have students compare and contrast words. Ask students to write a vocabulary word in each circle and list attributes for each word. Then have students write shared attributes in the common area shared by both circles. This organizational format will help students distinguish commonalities and differences in word meanings. An additional step can be added to have students summarize the similarities and differences. The example includes this extension of student word learning.

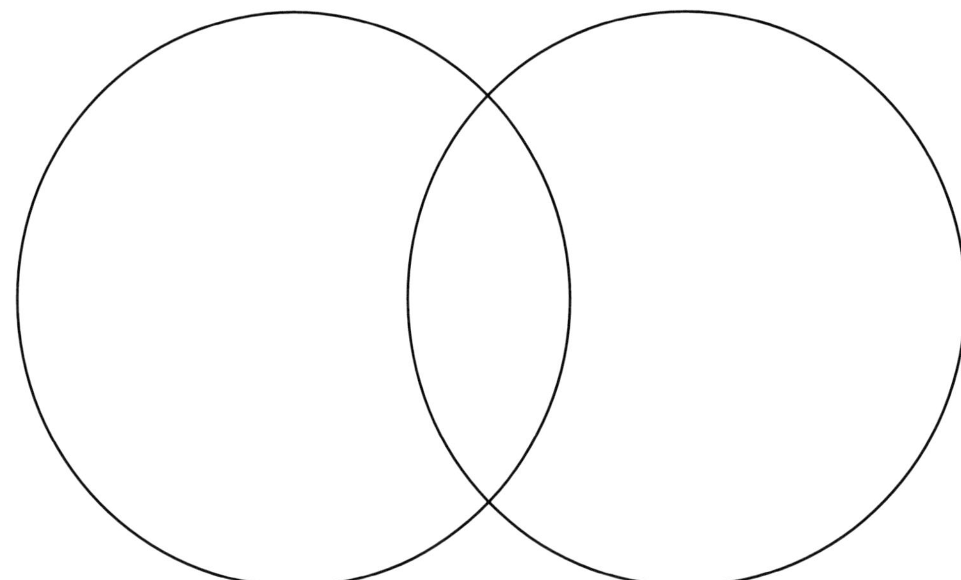

Example: Venn Diagram

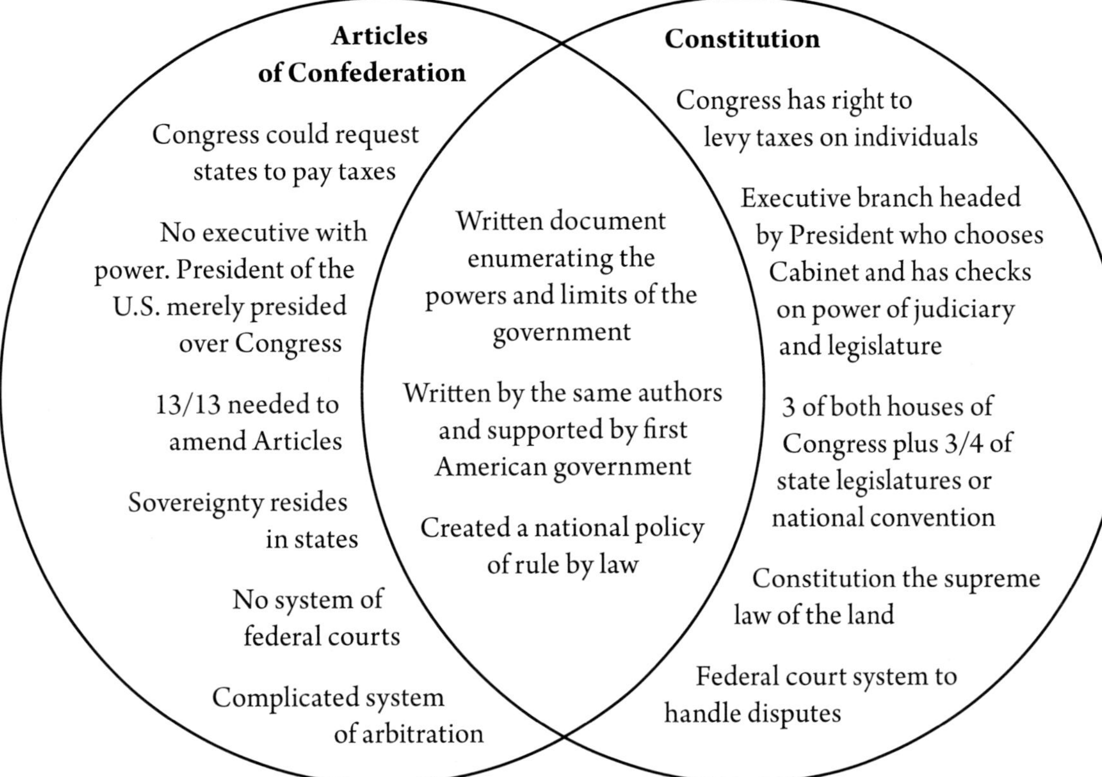

In the transition from the Articles to the Constitution the federal government gained more power creating a federalist state over a confederation of states. Reversing the focus of power from the states in the Articles of the Confederation, the centralization of power at the national level through delegated, reserved and enumerated powers were the cornerstone of the U.S. Constitution. Individual citizen rights were more clearly articulate in the Bill of Rights. A system of checks and balances was created among a three branch division to ensure rule by law.

T-charts

You can use the T-chart to have students examine two features of a particular concept or word. T-charts can show synonyms and antonyms as well as words associated with opposite sides of a concept. T-charts are also appropriate for common attributes/opposing attributes, cause/effect, and problem/solution text structures. Students can also use them to organize a personal response to a narrative or informational text. With this application, have students record the actual quote/summary on the left-hand side and a personal response, such as a question or connection, on the right side of the chart.

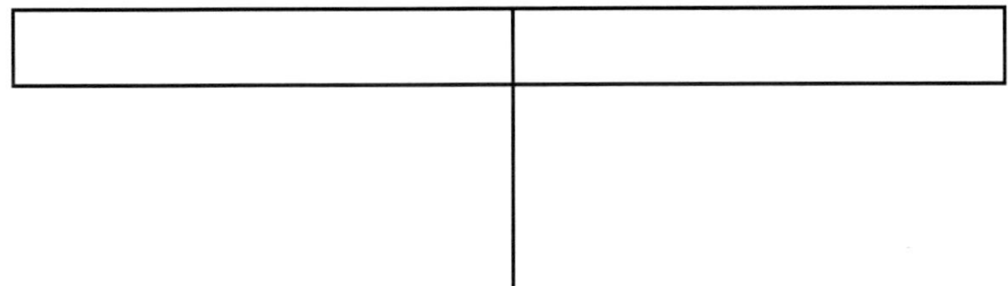

Example: T-Chart

Application 2: Continuum of Meaning

This strategy can be used both to develop conceptual thinking about content vocabulary as well as to reinforce basic meaning. *Continuum of Meaning* is especially useful for ELL students who often approach each vocabulary word as an isolated word to memorize and may not see the more subtle links and differences between words. It is also a great way to promote small group work and collaboration. To implement *Continuum of Meaning*, follow these steps:

1. Have students work in groups of three or four.

2. Provide the template and assign a focus word. Each group should be assigned a different word. To address the needs of all learners, you could have all groups develop a *Continuum of Meaning* for the same word. Students would then can compare their continuums at the end of the activity.

3. On one side, have students generate as many synonyms for the focal word as possible. On the other side, ask students to list antonyms.

4. Within their groups, have students arrange words in terms of strength.

5. Encourage students to discuss their rationale for their arrangements. The outcome of this explanatory process is for students to build a continuum of meanings ranging from words that have similar meaning to words that have opposite meanings. Based on their collaborative discussion they will be able to verbally describe their thinking.

6. Students should share their results with the class.

Continuum of Meaning Template

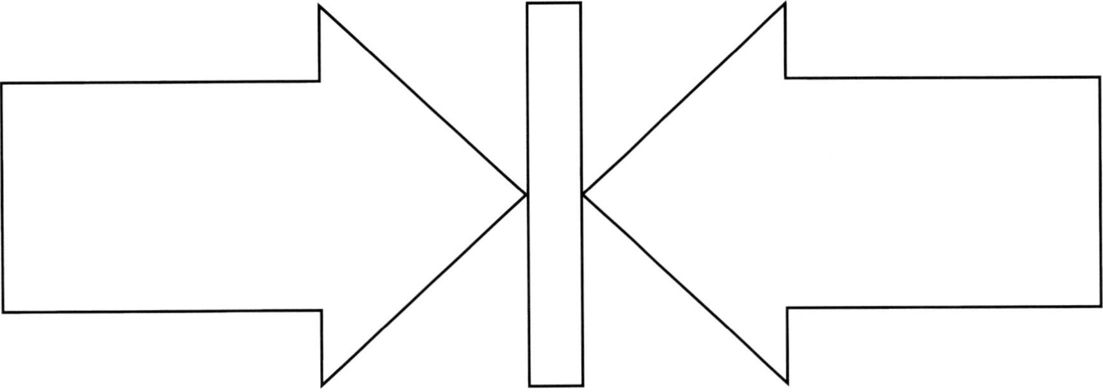

Example: Governmental Rule Continuum of Meaning

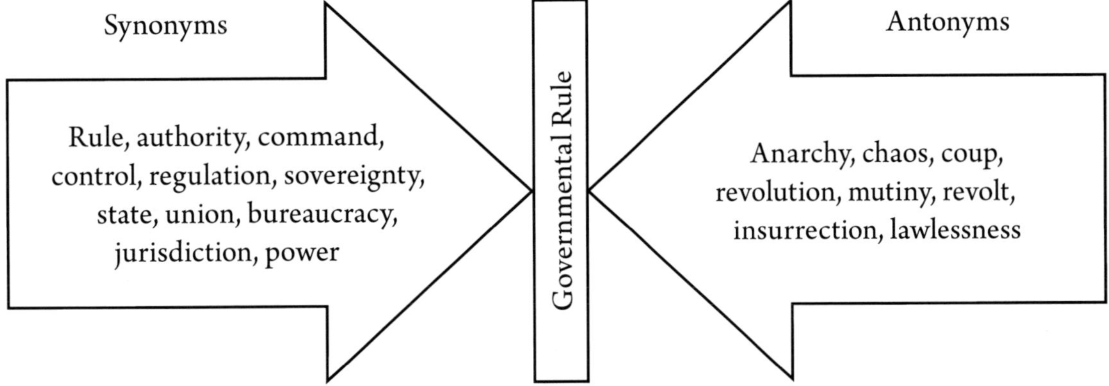

Example: Emancipation Continuum of Meaning

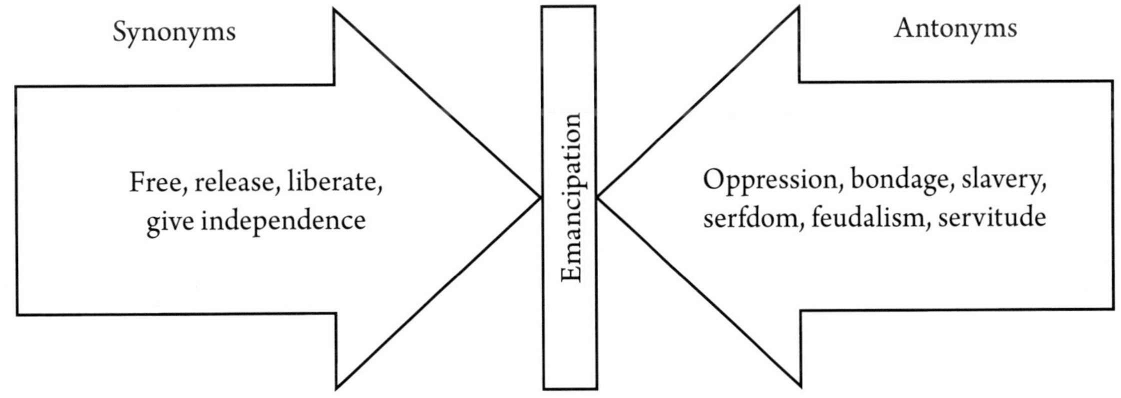

◎ Application 3: Relational Analysis

You can use *Relational Analysis* as a before- or during-reading activity to reinforce content concepts and target vocabulary. The semantic feature analysis allows students to compare and contrast the major tenets between words while reinforcing overall understanding. This strategy can also be used as an assessment of student word and content learning. To implement *Relational Analysis,* follow these steps:

1. Select similar and contrasting words from a word family and features related to the word family. List words down the left side of the template. List features across the top of the template.

2. Give students the template and ask them to read the text. As they read, they should place a mark in the intersection between each member of the word family and the features that have been identified.

   - A plus sign (+) indicates a relationship exists.

   - A minus sign (–) indicates the feature does not apply or there is no relationship.

3. Once students have completed the reading and template, ask students to give the word family a title.

4. Finally, students write a statement summarizing their findings about the relationships between the words and features.

Differentiation:

- Before they read, ask students to complete the feature analysis template in a particular color (blue pen, for example).

- Following their reading, they can complete the template in a separate color (green pen, for example).

- Ask students to reflect on the changes they made in their second pass.

Relational Analysis Template

Directions: Place a mark in the intersection between each member of the word family and the features that have been identified.

In the chart, place

- A plus sign (+) to indicate that a relationship exists between the column and row.

- A minus sign (−) to indicate that the feature does not apply or there is no relationship between the column and row.

Word Family: ____

Attribute / Word				

Explanation of Connections Among Words and Word Meanings:

____

____

Example: Types of Government Relational Analysis

Attribute / Word	Majority Rule	Egalitarian	Authoritarian	Rule by Few
Democracy	+	+	−	+
Oligarchy	−	−	+	+
Dictatorship	−	−	+	+
Republic	+	+	−	−

Example: Civil War Relational Analysis

Word Family Title: Politics and legislation leading to the Civil War

Attribute / Word	Supported Slavery	Supported States Rights	Peacemaking attempt between North and South	Legislation passed by Congress
Missouri Compromise of 1850	– +	–	+	+
Kansas-Nebraska Act of 1853	– +		–	+
Fugitive Slave Law	–			+
Freeport Doctrine	+	+	+	–

Explanation of Connections Among Words and Word Meanings:

The Kansas-Nebraska Act repealed the Missouri Compromise and represented further conflict between the Northern and Southern states. All of these events, except the Freeport Doctrine, were acts of Congress that angered one side or the other and led the country toward Civil War.

◉ Application 4: What Is It? What Is It Not?

This is a pre-, during-, or post-reading vocabulary activity that you can use to reinforce and review words and concepts, or you can use it to assess students' vocabulary mastery. This process is adapted from the attaining concepts model of teaching (Joyce, Weil, & Calhoun, 2009) and Allen's (1999) word development methods. To use the *What Is It? What Is It Not?* strategy, follow these steps:

1. Break the class into pairs or small groups. You can, however, implement this as an individual activity.

2. Give students a list of target vocabulary. All of the words must be things that can be illustrated and must possess an opposite meaning. If words cannot be illustrated, then students will use synonyms and antonyms.

3. Have students draw examples of what each word is and what it is not. Students may also seek examples (synonyms) and non-examples (antonyms) of the word in magazines or newspapers. Clip art is another resource for illustrations.

4. Remind students that they are not looking for the actual word, but rather a representation of the concept or the opposite of the concept.

5. Students write the synonyms and antonyms on a template or a T-chart. Student may also print clip art or cut out and glue the pictures in the template or on a sheet of paper. Three templates are included in the following descriptions to demonstrate variations that you can replicate with students.

Differentiation:

- Think-Pair-Share: Have students search for antonyms and/or synonyms independently. Then have students compare ideas with partners. Students can then add to the whole class template or share with the entire class. This modification is designed to help students expand word meanings.

- Pair-Share: Partner groups would look up different vocabulary words and share findings with the whole class as the class works collectively to create synonym and antonym lists for each word.

- Have students write a brief sentence stating why the pictures they chose are opposites or why they represent the words.

- Students can write a summary of what the words and their opposites have in common.

Example: Democracy/Democratic What Is It? What Is It Not?

Word or Concept: Democracy/Democratic	
What is the word or concept? What is it not? What are distinguishing facts about the word or concept or theme? What are non-traits or ways of identifying that these features do not belong to this word or concept?	
What is it? Characteristics that are unique or recognizable to this word or concept	*What is it not?* Qualities that are completely different from or contrary to the word or concept
People vote Majority rule Representatives elected Government by the people Legislative body Egalitarian Popular Republican Parliamentary Participatory Representative Classless	No voting A few rule Hereditary appointments Government by the best Centralized rule making Authoritarian Totalitarian Monarchical Despotic Dictatorial Despotic Autocratic
Definition: Democracy is a government of the people and by the people that is characterized by principles of social equality, representative rule, and participatory citizenship.	

Example: Apartheid What Is It? What Is It Not?

Word or Concept: Apartheid	
What is the word or concept? What is it not? What are distinguishing facts about the word or concept or theme? What are non-traits or ways of identifying that these features do not belong to this word or concept?	
What is it?	*What is it not?*
Segregation South Africa Disenfranchisement Jim Crow Laws *Plessy* v. *Ferguson* Racial and SES inequality Class or caste system Divisive Oppressive Feudalism	Desegregation Europe *Brown* v. *Board of Education* OAU (Organization of African Unity) Universal suffrage Equal rights Classless society Unifying Libertarian Democracy
Definition: A government that separates people based on race or caste and promotes a rigid policy of segregation.	

Example: Location Theory What Is It? What Is It Not?

Word or Concept: Location Theory	
What is it? Examples	*What is it not? Non-examples or Opposites*
A factory located near a mine that uses coal to fuel its machine	Supply and demand
Factory is near a train station with direct lines to market area it serves	Timber industry in a desert
Mill villages	Fishing industry in Kansas
Warehouses beside railroad tracks	Boat building in Nebraska
Crossing of major trade routes	
Position	
City locations, human settlements	
Definition: Location theory addresses important questions of who produces what goods and services in which locations and why.	

Templates: What is it? What is it not?

You can modify the format of the chart for *What Is It? What Is It Not?* to allow for differentiation. The next three templates demonstrate variations in organizational structure.

What is it? What is it not? T-Chart Template

Concept or Word	
Synonym	**Antonym**
Insert illustration or clip art	Insert illustration or clip art

Definition:

____

____

____

What is it? What is it not? Image Template

Directions: Using images, create examples of synonyms and antonyms for each word. You can use magazines, clip art, or draw your own images. When you have completed the chart, explain how these words relate to the overall concept. Then write a definition for the concept.

Concept: ____

Concept	Word	Word	Word	Word
What is it? **Synonym** **Antonym** *What is it not?*				

Summary:

____

____

____

____

Definition of Concept:

____

____

____

Adapted from Allen, J. (1999). *Words, words, words: Teaching vocabulary in grades 4–12.* York, ME: Stenhouse Publishers.

What Is It? What Is It Not? Linked Chart Template

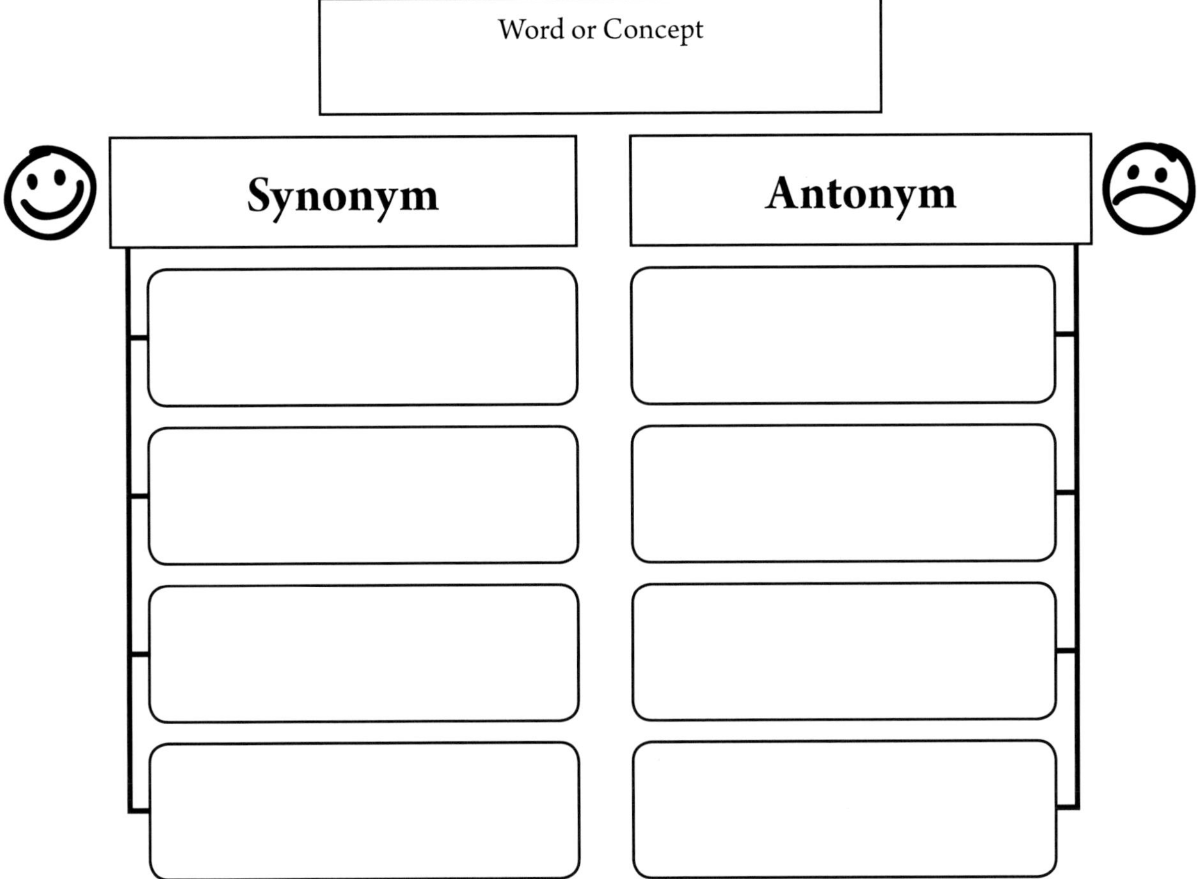

◎ Instructional Routine 3: Summary

Comparing and Contrasting words helps deepen students' understanding of an overall concept or unit topical focus. It allows students to move beyond an initial familiarity with the words they encounter, to unpack word meanings needed to increase comprehension. This process is an extension of the first two instructional routines. Drawing upon the benefits of understanding words through other words, the strategies presented in the third instructional routine use antonyms and synonyms to promote cumulative word learning. Such comparisons require students to build academic vocabulary from a variety of sources. Through *Comparing and Contrasting*, students develop a more complex knowledge of social studies words and word meanings. Increased vocabulary knowledge builds background knowledge and support content comprehension. Further, as students learn to compare and contrast meanings, they are better prepared to transfer this process to other content and generate their own vocabulary learning. The deeper levels of word awareness that students develop in this instructional routine prepare students for the next exposure to word learning: *Defining and Associating*.

INSTRUCTIONAL ROUTINE 4: DEFINING AND ASSOCIATING

Applications

1. Vocabulary Manipulative Cards (VMC)

2. Tiered Word Sorts

3. Sorting Degrees of Knowledge

4. Forced Associations

5. Squared Up

6. Personal Vocabulary Journals (PVJs)

7. Word of the Day

8. Contextual Cues

9. Roll the Die

10. Concept Associations

11. Memory Aids and Mnemonics

In-depth knowledge of content-specific words

Words and meanings through associations

Process of discovering more about word meanings

The instructional activities described in the first three chapters ask students to consider words in connection to one another. The benefit of these applications is that they guide students to consider multiple words at the same time. However, these activities may not provide the nuanced understanding of content-specific words that students encounter in social studies texts. It is important to provide students with the opportunities to gain in-depth knowledge of some words. The number of words that you can cover with this level of depth is much fewer than you can cover with strategies described in the first three instructional routines, making the choice of words important. Further, you should never turn these activities into rote-memory tasks.

One important way of moving the task away from rote memorization is to involve students in the process of discovering more about the meanings of words. Concept associations introduce students to etymologies of words and often allows for discussion about the history of a particular time, people, or place and the way language reflects history. The *Squared Up* activity helps students identify not just a definition, but synonyms and antonyms associated with a word. This capitalizes on a key principle of teaching vocabulary while maximizing the effectiveness of instructional time—don't teach a single word when multiple words can be connected and taught simultaneously. Synonyms and antonyms help students nuance their understanding of the word. The additional activities provide further variations of complex word learning strategies.

Memory aids can have a positive impact on word learning. Memory aids do not include memorization through repetition, but rather systematic learning, specifically, mnemonic strategies such as picture-word associations, rhyming, chunking, link word, and forced associations. These are inductive thinking methods whereby students group information into categories to create symbolic associations. The key to vocabulary learning success is having students make connections so that learning is not by repetition but rather by association. Students who master material more quickly and who retain it longer generally use more elaborate strategies, like mnemonics, for memorizing material. Less effective memorizers generally use "rote" procedures; they "say" what is to be memorized and believe it will stay there. The more associations made, the better students will retain information as cognitive activity increases (Joyce, Weil, & Calhoun, 2009). Memory aids also extend the number of exposures students have with words and multiple pathways to learning words.

As students use these strategies, ask these comprehension questions:

1. What does this word mean?

2. How did this word acquire this meaning?

3. What associations can be made with this word?

◎ Application 1: Vocabulary Manipulative Cards (VMCs)

Vocabulary Manipulative Cards (VMCs) are flash cards that allow students to work with and manipulate words to develop vocabulary understanding. *VMCs* provide students with an independent way of reviewing the terms. They can use the cards as a study tool during a unit of study and share them as a collaborative activity when games are used to review *VMCs*. To use *VMCs*:

1. Students write the target word on one side of a note card. On the other side they write or illustrate the word's meaning. They can use symbols and images to support mnemonic learning rather than rote memorization.

2. Students can also create a stack of word cards and a separate stack of illustrated meanings.

3. Have students record words and concepts on different colored index cards. For example, students can separate the four divisions of words (see *Tiered Word Sorts* for more information) into basic (blue), general (orange), content-specific (green), and overarching (yellow).

4. Students then "play" with the *VMCs*. With minor adaptations, you can use flash cards for games such as *Rummy, Memory, Matching,* and *Go Fish*. Instructional Routine 5 offers more games in which students review and play with play words.

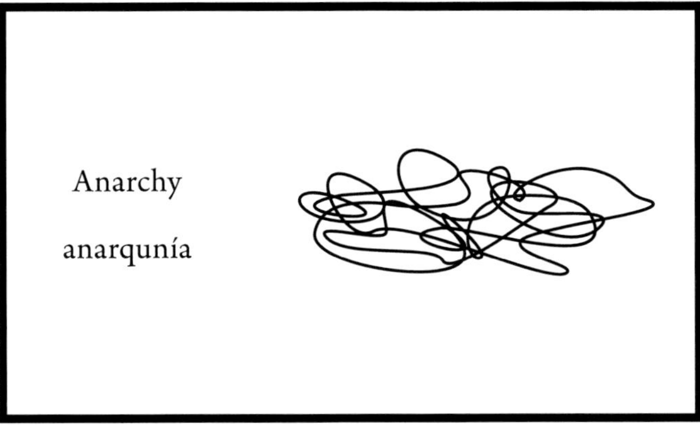

Differentiated Strategies for VMCs:

- Antonym cards: Students write the word and its meaning on one side, and on the other they write an antonym.

- Picture cards: Students write the word and its meaning on one side, and on the other they draw an illustration.

- Iconic Images cards: Students identify iconic images of historical significance that are associated with each word. They write the word and definition on one side and the iconic image on the other side.

- Mnemonic cards: Students write the word and its meaning on one side, and on the other they put a mnemonic association.

- ELL cards: ELL students write the English word and its meaning on one side, and on the other they write the word in their native language.

- Significance cards: Students write the word on one side, and on the other they write the word's significance to the current unit of study.

Examples: VMCs: Antonym Cards and ELL Cards

Antonym Cards:

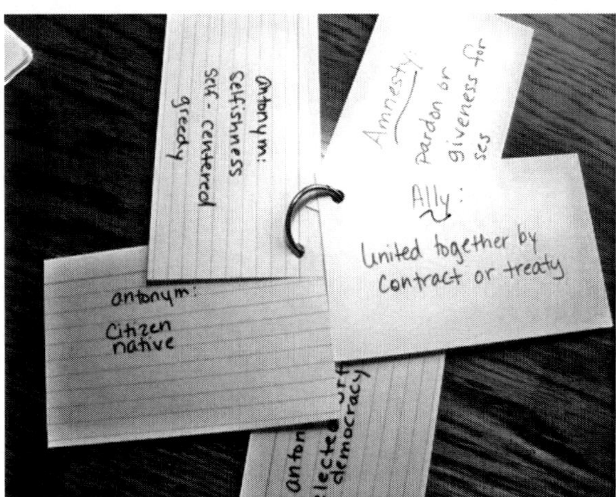

ELL Cards:

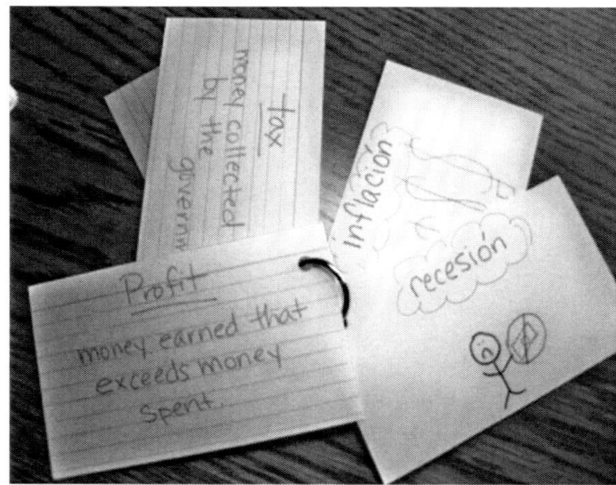

Differentiated Processes:

- Students can create flipbooks instead of flash cards. Students stack the paper, staggering the top by 1 inch. They then fold the stack in half, creating a book with graduated distance between each of the pages. (They can cut these books in half to create two books and conserve paper, if desired.)

- Students put a target word on each of the flaps and write the definition on the inside of each one. They can add picture cues and mnemonic cues can.

Example: VMCs: Flipbooks

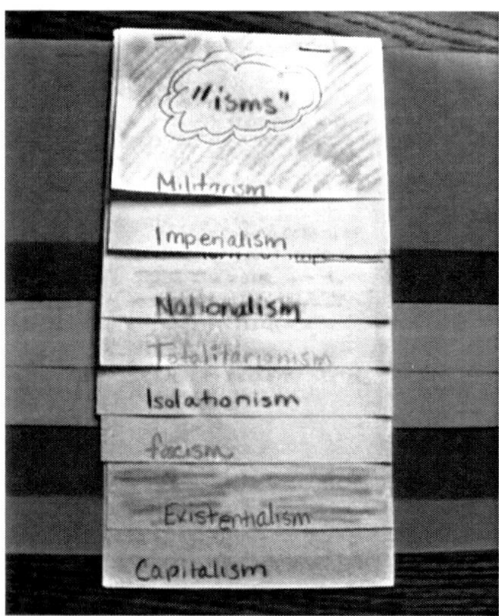

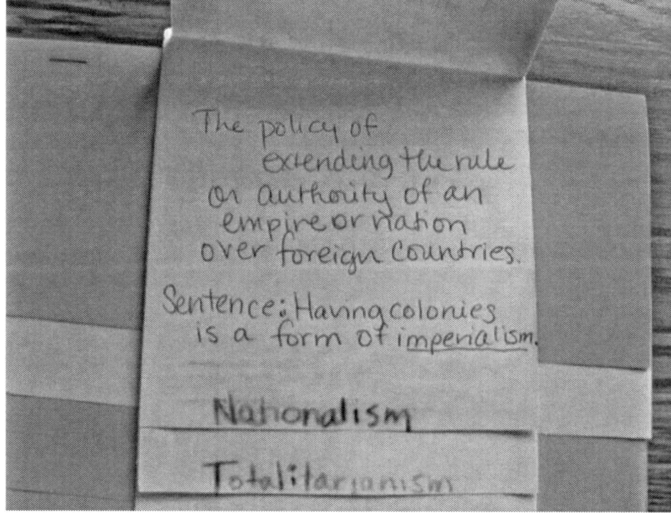

Differentiated Processes:

- Students can create flipbooks instead of flash cards. Students stack the paper, staggering the top by 1 inch. They then fold the stack in half, creating a book with graduated distance between each of the pages. (You can cut these books in half to create two books and conserve paper, if you like.)

- Students put a target word on each of the flaps and write the definition on the inside of each one. They can add picture cues and mnemonic cues.

- Audio cards: Using *Audacity.com* (http://audacity.sourceforge.net/) or any audio recording file including PowerPoint®, you or your students can create flash cards that have accompanying word pronunciations and readings of word meanings.

- You or students can create flash cards online using many free programs such as http://www.kitzkikz.com/flashcards/.

- You or students can go to *Quizlet.com* (http://quizlet.com) and use existing flash cards with words, word meanings, and audio files. (For example, see http://quizlet.com/3344265/social-studies-forms-of-government-flash-cards/.)

◎ Application 2: Tiered Word Sorts

As you teach social studies vocabulary, you will become more aware of how students learn words of varying familiarity and difficulty. In instructional routines 1–3 you discovered strategies that help students learn words through interconnected and relational approaches. Tiered Word Sorts builds on these methods and presents a progressive approach to word learning. To use this strategy, begin with simpler ideas, such as words students are familiar with or words that could be easy to learn. Once learners gain word awareness, then progress to more complex content-specific terminology.

You can also use a tiered approach to sort word lists for indentifying appropriate vocabulary strategies and techniques to build word consciousness and conceptual thinking. Typically, word lists for units are often arranged either alphabetically or topically. Sorting vocabulary word lists into tiers based on word difficulty will help students recognize the level of exposures they will need to learn new words. This will also give students clues as to what strategies would be more appropriate for tiered word learning. You will want to sort your word lists into four tiers: basic, content specific, abstract, and overarching.

Each tier contains specific categories of words. Basic words are words that are important in multiple disciplines, not just social studies. These words may contain Greek and Latin elements that help students generate knowledge of new words, or they may be common words and/or labels that are used in a specific way within social studies. Prefixes, suffixes, and root words along with word origins are helpful in expanding common and frequently used vocabulary. An example of a tier one vocabulary list could be *man* or *manu*, meaning "by hand" and found as the root word of common social studies vocabulary such as manufacture, manual, manicure, and manifest.

Tier two sorts content specific words that are considered foundational to social studies. These words reflect the Common Core Standards and the National Council for Social Studies' goals as they relate to social studies content. They include documents, legislation, events, people/groups, places, and structures.

In continuing the example of man/manu, social studies specific words such as manucaption (document in court), manacles (handcuffs), or manumit (to release from contract). Expanding on this last concept, social studies specific words, such as emancipate or Emancipation Proclamation, find similar root word origins. Categorical associations could include Abraham Lincoln, the Civil War, or the Civil Rights Act of 1964.

Abstract words are words or phrases that reference complex ideas, or ideas that are defined using several words. These concepts are often groups of words and terms. Examples would be the abolition of slavery, U.S. Civil War abolitionists, Constitutional Amendments 13, 14, and 15.

Overarching words are those big ideas and broad themes that have cross disciplinary currents. They make connections among the various disciplines that define the social studies as well as between social studies and other disciplines. Concepts of social justice, identity formation, universal human rights, civil disobedience, equality, or civil rights are examples. These could also be specific to other subject areas such as comparisons among the American Civil Rights Movement, Mahatma Gandhi's writings on civil disobedience, and the Universal Declaration of Rights.

The following chart shows examples of the four tiers of words and how the tiers help establish a hierarchical understanding of the broader concept.

Word Type	Category	Code
Basic	Roots	Roots
	Common Words	Common
	Labels/Tags	Labels
Content Specific	Documents/Legislations	Docs
	Events	Events
	People/Groups	People
	Places	Places
	Structures	Structures
Abstract	Content Concepts	Content
	General Concepts	General
Overarching	Big Ideas	Big Ideas

Example: Tiered Word Sorts

Word	Tier/Category	Word	Tier/Category
imperialism	Content Concepts	Isaac Newton	People
impressionism	Content Concepts	Islam	Content Concepts
Indian and Muslim	Content Concepts	isolationism	Content Concepts
Indo-Europeans	Groups	Italian Renaissance	Events
inductive reasoning	Common Words	Mao Zedong	People
Industrial Revolution	Events	market economy	Content Concepts
innovation	Common Words	Martin Luther	People
Inquisition	Events	mass production	Content Concepts
interdependence	Content Concepts	Middle Passage	Places
Internet	Common Words	migration	Content Concepts
intifada	Events	Miguel Hidalgo	People
Iron Curtain	Content Concepts	militarism	Content Concepts
irrigation	Common Words	Mohandas Gandhi	People
Monroe Doctrine	Docs	monarchy	Structures
monsoons	LabelsTags	money economy	Content Concepts

◎ Application 3: Sorting Degrees of Knowledge

A variation of *Degrees of Knowledge* is to have students use *Vocabulary Manipulative Cards (VMCs)* to sort words based on their understanding of the meaning of the words. This strategy uses similar processes of *Degrees of Knowledge* but rather than writing words, students would use either their created *VMCs* or laminated word cards you developed. The strategy works well to introduce words at the beginning of the unit. Students can then determine what words they already know (a measure of prior knowledge for you) and recognize what words they are going to have to spend time learning. This recognition will help you and your students identity vocabulary strategies that will develop the level of word awareness needed to understand the unknown and less familiar words. The ability to sort these words over and over allows you to use this strategy not just as a word introduction activity, but multiple times throughout a unit. In this capacity, *Sorting Degrees of Knowledge* becomes a tool for ongoing, formative assessment of student word learning. Students can also use this activity to self-assess word understanding. As you progress through a unit of study, students' confidence in knowing word meanings should increase.

HOW WELL DO I KNOW THE MEANING OF WORDS?

Name ____   Date _________________________

Directions: Using the collection of Vocabulary Manipulative Cards (VMCs), sort words into groups based on your confidence in how well you know each word. First, select a word from your stack of words. After you read each word, place it into a group with the heading that best describes what you know about the word.

I know a meaning.

I think I know the meaning.

I have seen or heard it, but I don't know the meaning.

I don't know it at all.

Degrees of Knowledge

Word List:

◎ Application 4: Forced Associations

The *Forced Associations* strategy draws on the use of similes to teach and review word meanings. It combines two things that do not go together. It is a great tool for interdisciplinary teaching and helping students formalize cross-curricular connections. You can use *Forced Associations* to introduce vocabulary words early in a unit or to review words at the end of an instructional unit. The process is also appropriate as a pre-reading or post-reading strategy when accompanied by a text. *Forced Associations* works well with all types of vocabulary words but is especially applicable with concepts. To implement this strategy, follow these steps:

1. Select a target vocabulary word and a second unrelated word.

2. Ask students to write a simile about the word (a comparison using the words *like* or *as*): How is ____________ like ____________? The emphasis in each statement is on similarities of the two concepts. Students will need a solid understanding of both words in the *Forced Association*. If students struggle with the comparison, have them review the definitions of each word. It is from the attributes of each word meaning that links are made through the use of *Forced Associations*.

3. Review each *Forced Association*. Have students explain their comparisons. They should use word definitions and examples to explain the meaning of each comparison.

4. They can repeat this process for other targeted words.

Differentiated Process:

- As a variation, you could have students brainstorm possible words to create a forced association.

- You can select words from earlier units of study or other disciplines. If you use words from other disciplines, try cross-curricular collaboration with content area teachers to ensure that you use accurate word meanings.

- Rather than asking students to think of similes, you can provide *Forced Association* statements and then ask students to explain the connections between words.

- *Forced Association* can be a whole-class process, used in small groups, or assigned as an individual task. If you ask students to make forced associations individually, we recommend using the process as vocabulary review or as an assessment of student word learning.

- You could also use *VMCs* as manipulatives for creating *Forced Associations*.

Forced Associations with VMCs

As students gain familiarity with *Forced Associations*, *VMCs* can be added as a way for students to review vocabulary. *Forced Associations with VMCs* is also a valuable way to assess student understanding of targeted vocabulary.

- Create a stack of cards, writing a target vocabulary word on each one.

- Create a second set containing unrelated words randomly generated from another subject area students are studying.

- Place students in small groups and have the first student choose a card from each stack.

- Have students consider their knowledge of both terms and generate one sentence that describes a way in which the two terms are similar.

- Have students record their responses on a sheet of notebook paper and allow them to choose and share their most creative response with the entire class.

Example: Forced Associations with VMCs

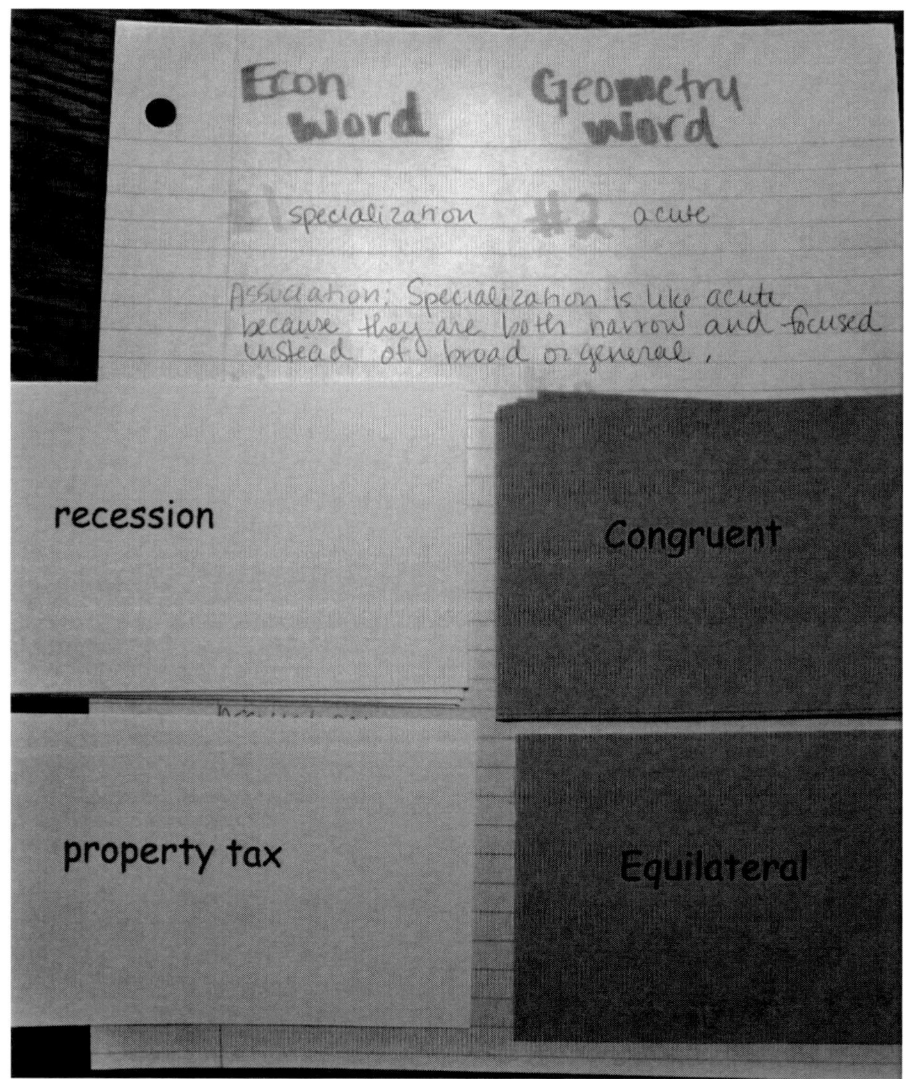

Example: Forced Associations: Democracy

How is Democracy like an equilateral triangle?

Democracy   **Equilateral Triangle**

The example asks students to make a *Forced Association* between democracy, a social studies vocabulary concept, and equilateral triangle, a math topic. How is democracy like an equilateral triangle? Students might make the following statements about the similarities between the two:

- Democracy has equal participation by all citizens. An equilateral triangle has equal sides.

- In American democracy, there are three branches of government that share and balance the distribution of governmental power. An equilateral triangle has three equal angles and three equal sides of the same length.

- No matter how big or small a country is, the people rule in a democracy. No matter how big or small an equilateral triangle is, all sides and angles will be equal.

- In an American democracy, governmental powers are divided among national, state, and local governments. Equilateral triangles are bilaterally symmetrical. You can draw a line down the middle and both sides will be equal and this can be done in three different ways.

◎ Application 5: Squared Up

This is a pre-reading or during-reading activity that students can do in class or as homework, with the group component taking place in the classroom. *Squared Up* draws on the use of synonyms and antonyms as well as in-text word-learning strategies to build student understanding of target vocabulary. To implement this strategy, follow these steps:

1. Have students prepare one card for each of the target words.

2. Then, in the middle of each card ask them to write a target word and alternate forms of the word.

3. Have students read the text. Direct them to identify word use and meaning as they read. On each card, on the two squares to the left, guide students to list a definition and sentence from the text.

4. As they read, students identify synonyms and antonyms as a way to further define the attributes and non-attributes of the target word. On the cards, in the two squares to the right, the students produce a synonym and an antonym and a list of other words associated with the target word.

5. Have students place a visual representation of each target word on the back of each card.

Differentiation:

- Students needing an extra challenge can add two squares, one in which they build an analogy using the word and the other in which they write possible exam questions.

- ELLs can add a native language translation in place of or in addition to the alternate word forms.

- Students can create and store the cards in a Web-based note card system, such as *MuseumBox.com, Prezi.com,* or another online flash card tool.

Web Tools

Students can use the following sites for making and storing flash cards:

- *MuseumBox.com:* http://museumbox.e2bn.org/

- *Prezi.com:* http://prezi.com/

- *Free Printable Flash Card Maker:* http://www.kitzkikz.com/flashcards/

- *FlashcardExchange.com:* http://www.flashcardexchange.com/

- *Quizlet.com:* http://quizlet.com/

Students can use these site to find antonyms and synonyms:

- *Synonym.com:* http://www.synonym.com/ and http://www.synonym.com/antonym/

- *Synonym.org:* http://www.synonym.org/synonym/

- *Dictionary.com:* http://dictionary.reference.com/browse/antonym

- *Thesaurus.com:* http://thesaurus.com/

Template: Squared Up

Front of card:

Definition:	Word:	Synonyms:
	Other forms of the word:	**Antonyms:**
Sentence from the text:		**Other words associated with the word:**

Back of card:

Illustration/Picture:

Example: Squared Up for Catholicism

Front of card:

Definition: Religion associated with belief in Jesus Christ, confession of sin, doing good works	**Word:** Catholicism **Other forms of the word:** catholic, catholicize	**Synonyms:** Christian **Antonyms:**
Sentence from the text: The Spanish also brought Catholicism to the New World. (p. 21)		**Other words associated with the word:** church, pope, bishop, priest, nun, Vatican, missionary, Roman Catholic Church, rosary, crucifix

Back of card:

Illustration/Picture:

Example: Squared Up for Religion

Religion is the key topic for this unit. However, the word itself has many connotations. One of the first activities of the unit should be to explore what the word actually means.

Front of card:

Definition: a set of beliefs concerning the cause, nature, and purpose of the universe, especially when considered as the creation of a superhuman agency or agencies, usually involving devotional and ritual observances, and often containing a moral code governing the conduct of human affairs	**Word:** religion **Other forms of the word:** religious, religiosity	**Synonyms:** devotion, doctrine, orthodoxy, fundamentalism, spiritual **Antonyms:** agnosticism, atheism
Sentence from the text: The origin, doctrines, and practices of religious groups affects society, culture, and individual personality. (p. 12)		**Other words associated with the word:** church, messiah, holy book, eternal, afterlife

Back of card:

Illustration/Picture: 

New York Avenue Presbyterian Church, Washington, DC

Squared Up Foldable

For a more interactive activity, have students create a *Squared Up Foldable*. Follow the same steps for *Squared Up*. To make the foldable, students should fold the corners of a square piece of paper. Dotted lines on the template demonstrate how the paper should be folded. For an example of what the foldable should look like, refer to the acculturation example presented for Squares and Roots.

Squared Up Foldable Template

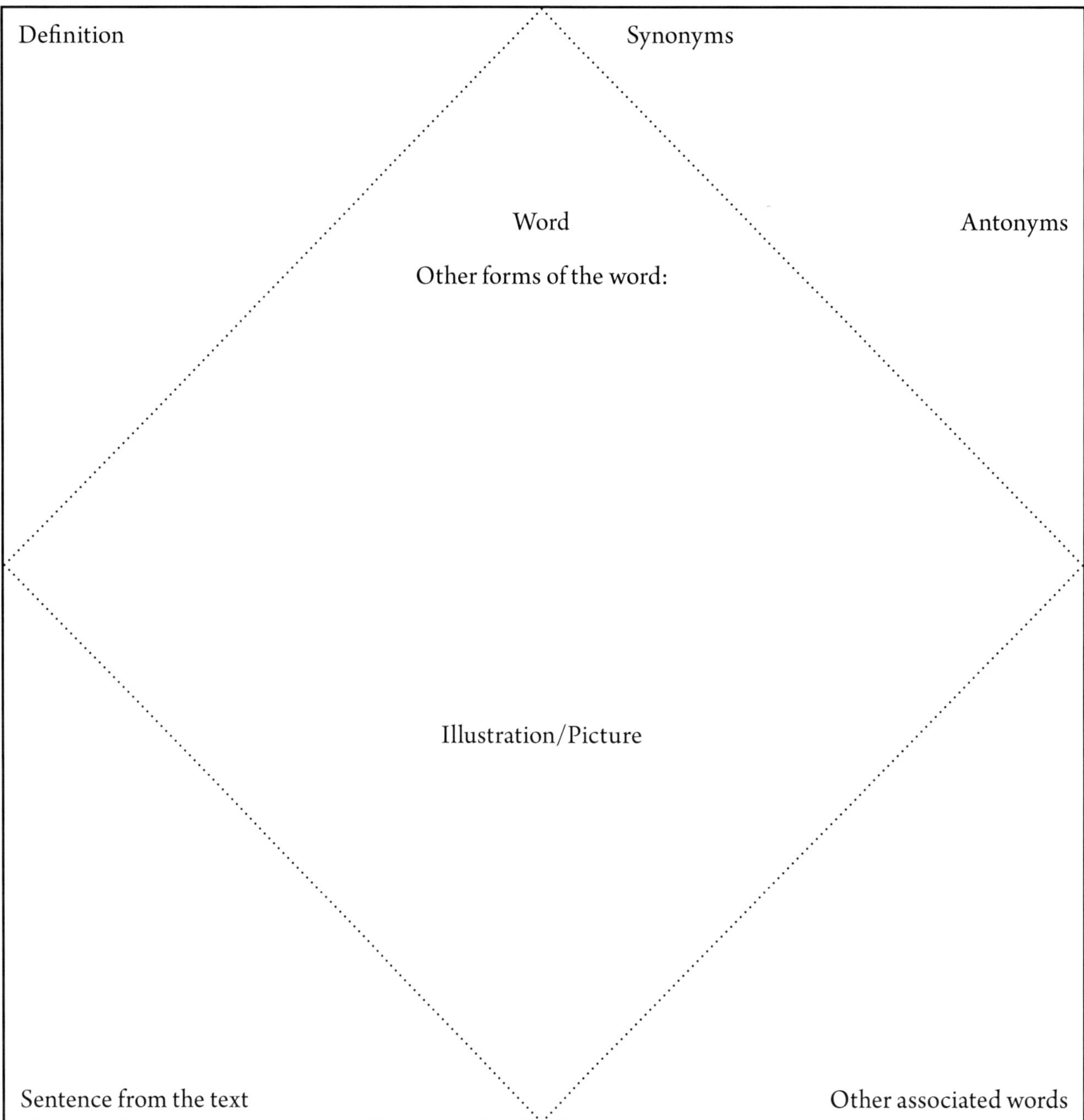

◉ Application 6: Personal Vocabulary Journals (PVJs)

Personal Vocabulary Journals (PVJs) are student-created vocabulary learning tools. You can use this as a pre-, during-, or post-reading activity to initiate target word learning as well as reinforce and review key vocabulary. *PVJs* are also a good follow-up student strategy to the personal *Word Wall.* To implement this strategy:

1. Have students maintain a vocabulary notebook throughout a unit of study. Hand out the template on page 113 and tell them that they can re-create it any number of times in their journals. Then assign a list of vocabulary words that you have pre-selected.

2. Guide students to locate the target words in their readings and complete the elements of the *PVJ* template. They should generate definitions based on what they read in the textbook, the assigned text reading (such as a primary source document), or an Internet source you designate.

3. This activity should focus on a shorter list of words that are unfamiliar to students. Students need additional interactions with these words to become conscious of word meanings. To ensure that students have a minimum of twelve interactions with the words throughout a unit, use this strategy early in the unit.

4. As a form of review, play games with the words students record in their *PVJs.* Instructional Routine 5 will provide you with various vocabulary games that are applicable with *PVJs.*

Differentiation:

The following are variations of *PVJs* that will help you meet the needs of all learners:

- Word Detective: Ask students to find a given number of unfamiliar words in each assigned reading. They can then define these words as homework, bring them to class and discuss them as a whole group, or define them in pairs with a peer. Students can compare lists to see if they have duplicate entries.

- Word Mapping: Give students a template that they can re-create any number of times in their journals. Then assign students a pre-selected list of vocabulary words. They must locate the words in their readings and complete the elements of the template.

- Two-way Journal: Ask students to maintain a list of difficult vocabulary. Have them fold a page of their journals in half. On one side, they write your definition of the target word. On the other side, they write a definition in their own words, adding a personal association.

- Picture Dictionary: Have students write the target vocabulary in their journals and then create a visual representation of the word to demonstrate their comprehension.

- Sourcing Journals: Students write the word and its definition and where they found the definition. Students can add pictures of words.

Examples: Personal Vocabulary Journals

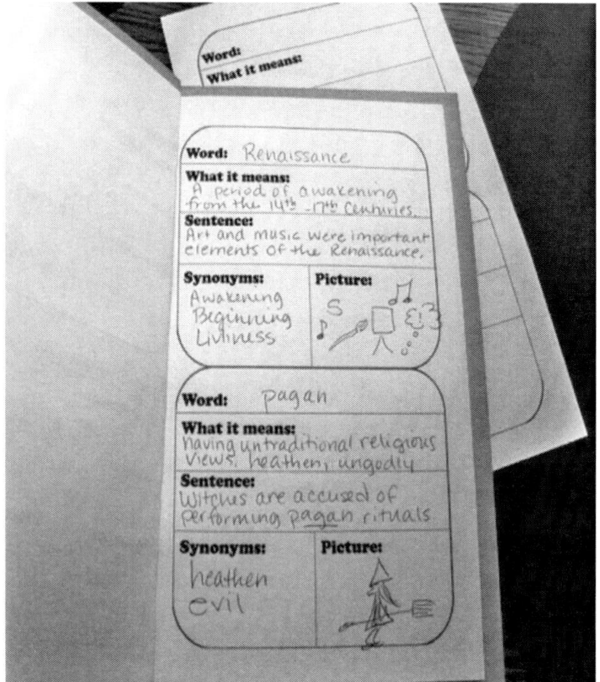

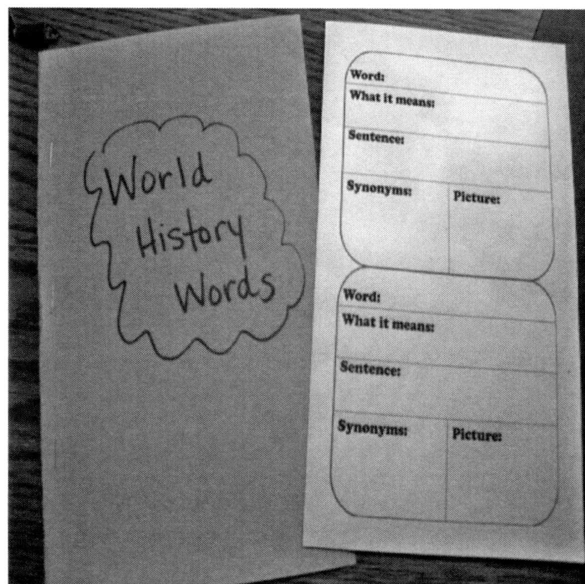

Example: Judicial Review Personal Vocabulary Journal Entry

Word:	
judicial review	
Definition:	
power of court to decide the constitutionality of government laws and acts	
Sentence:	
The Supreme Court exercised the power of judicial review in *Marbury* v. *Madison*.	
Synonym:	**Picture:**
legal constitutional authority	

Personal Vocabulary Journals Template

Word:

Definition:

Sentence:

Synonym:

Picture:

Word:

Definition:

Sentence:

Synonym:

Picture:

Word:

Definition:

Sentence:

Synonym:

Picture:

Word:

Definition:

Sentence:

Synonym:

Picture:

◎ Application 7: Word of the Day

You can use the *Word of the Day* strategy throughout a given unit of study. A bulletin board is a great way to display the *Word of the Day* and reinforce word learning throughout a lesson. You can introduce the *Word of the Day* as a preview assignment at the beginning of a lesson or integrate it in the lesson review as an exit ticket or ticket out the door. To use *Word of the Day*, follow these steps:

1. Establish a *Word of the Day* and display it.

2. At the beginning of each class period, model a word study of the target word. Display the word and the part of text where the students will see the word.

3. Use the word throughout the lecture, stopping to emphasize its use and context each time.

4. Throughout the class, encourage students to use the word.

5. Extend the understanding of the word by referencing other forms of the word. For example, link the word *glacier* with *glacial* to maximize students' recognition of the multiple forms of the word.

6. Have students restate and review the meaning of the *Word of the Day* at the end of the class. Students should share examples of how the word was used in the day's content.

Differentiation:

- Have students maintain an ongoing list of daily words, creating a word bank and resource for students to use in class discussions.

- Give bonus points to students you catch using the word properly during class discussions or when asking questions.

- Use a class signal (whistle, clap, cheer, etc.) to emphasize the use of past and current daily words.

Example: Census Word of the Day

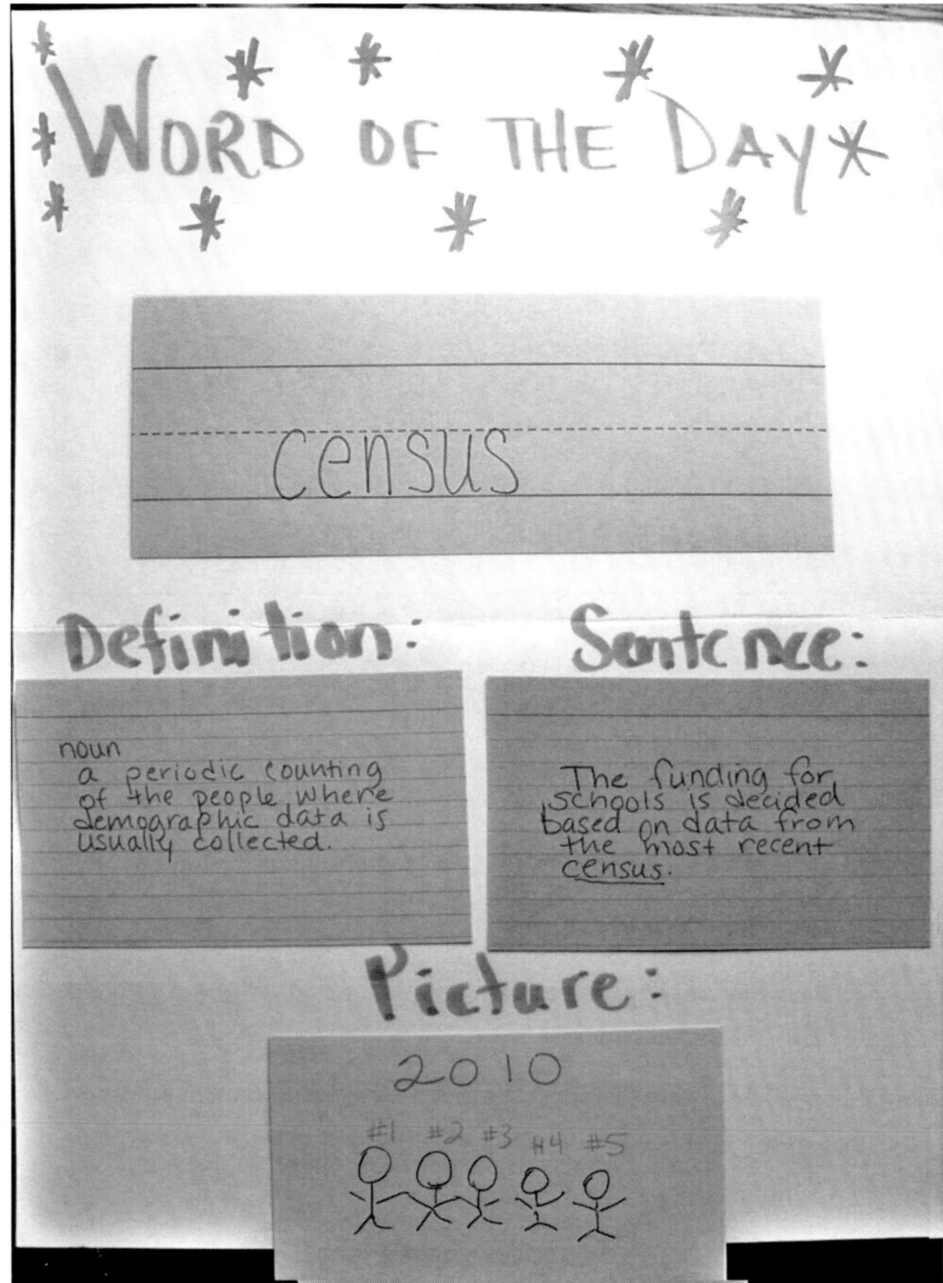

Example: Sit-Ins Word of the Day

Use *Word of the Day* to cover the key leaders, organizations, legislation, and cases during the American Civil Rights movement.

Word of the Day	Sit-ins Historical Event: Greensboro Sit-ins
Definition	• Form of protest, passive resistance and civil disobedience to inflict economic hardship on discriminatory agencies • Led by student groups and organizations, such as the youth movement within the NAACP • In Greensboro, North Carolina, NCA&T State University, Bennett College, Dudley High School, and Greensboro Women's College (later to become UNC Greensboro), students maintained the protest. The Greensboro Sit-in sparked widespread protest across the state and South.
Sentence	While the Sit-in Movement was mostly a southern movement, it brought national attention to social and economic inequalities of African Americans. The sit-in protests were successful because of the economic losses that store owners experienced, and it resulted in integration of public and private spaces.

◎ Application 8: Contextual Clues

Contextual Clues is an activity that you can use pre- or post-reading to support and assess students' vocabulary comprehension. The activity will raise student awareness of the importance of context clues in determining word meaning. To implement *Contextual Clues*, follow these steps:

1. Identify approximately ten target vocabulary words taken out of context and distribute the template that follows below.

2. Have students guess the words' meanings.

3. Place students in groups to complete the template by locating the word and reading in context.

4. Ask students to identify which type of context clues support their predictions.

   a. Synonyms/antonyms

   b. Local context

   c. Structural analysis

   d. Background knowledge

   e. Global context

Differentiation:

- Students reflect on what they have learned using context clues.

- Ensure that English Language Learners (ELLs) are utilizing their native language by looking for clues in the form of cognates.

- Pair ELLs with bilingual classmates. Include cognates and native language translation as part of their assignment.

Contextual Clues Template

Work with a group to make predictions for definitions of each of the following words. The words included here are found in ________________. Remember that some words that look familiar will probably have new meanings in this context.

Word	**Predict the Definition from the Word** *(Clues to use: word parts, picture clues, prior knowledge)*	**Predict the Definition from the Context** *(Use the sentence and paragraph to revise your definition.)*	**Actual Definition**
What clues did you use to determine word meanings?			

Contextual Clues Template Variation

The template can be modified to meet your needs and to align with the text reading. This modification added the layer of Tiered Word Sorts by having students identify word-level clues.

Word	Word-level clues	Context clues	Predicted Word Meaning	Actual Word Meaning
	Clue:	Clue:		
	Clue:	Clue:		
	Clue:	Clue:		

Example: VMCs Contextual Clues

Students can use *VMCs* to identify words from informational texts. When using *Contextual Clues*, students formulate a definition based on the context clues. Then students verify the accuracy of the word meaning using another source. Next, students draw an image of the word as a visualization strategy and mnemonic device.

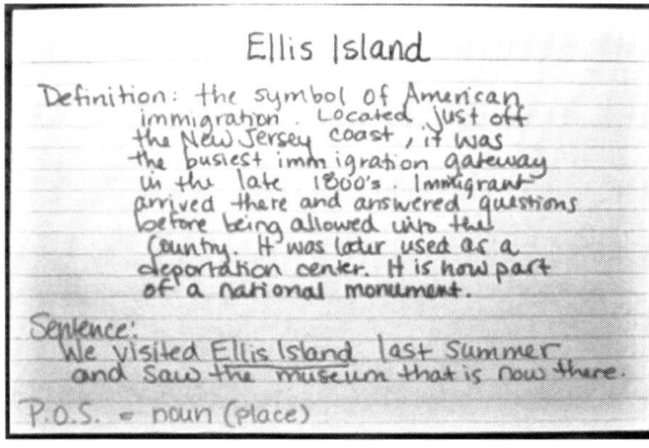

Example: Reading for Contextual Clues

This is a during-reading exercise where students were given a world history text reading and asked to highlight unknown words they encountered as they read. Students then identified contextual clues, guessed what the word might mean, and then checked their thinking with a secondary source.

Jnion of Socialist Sovi...
cal environment. No other conflict of interest
War Two world like the cold war did. One man is
ld war, Mikhail Gorbachev. This however was not the
is responsible for. The end of the cold war was just a
jor event he was involved with. That is the fall of
d the collapse of the USSR itself.

st reformer was appointed General Secretary of the
iet Union in 1985. His appointment followed the death
ders in three years. Leonid Brezhnev was first to go
nd Konstantin Chernenko. Not being able to afford
he old guard appointed the youthful 56 year old Mikhial
tary.

eemed as if this great superpower self-destructed in
GR's demise is of course more complicated than this.
an be traced back to Gorbachevs appointment and his
troduced a wide ranging program of reform. His major
estroika and democratization. These reforms allowed
to be uncovered and become public knowledge.

mic inefficiency and historical atrocities were the maj
d. How he dealt with these challenges and how
ed in this report.

Unknown Word	Clues	Guess	Check
Mikhail Gorbachev	it's a name! "man" "USSR"	Russian Leader	✓
old gaurd	none ☺	?	the government authority in the USSR that represent traditional values
reforms	"early" he was new	changes	✓
glasnost	No idea!	No idea!	policy of openess + transparency
democratization	-ization on process of becoming democracy	Becoming a democracy	✓
atrocities	the passage talks about challenges	something bad?	extreme wicked

◉ Application 9: Roll the Die

Roll the Die is a pre-reading or during-reading activity that you can do entirely in class or assign for homework, following up by doing the group component in the classroom. You can also use it as a *Review and Play* activity with Instructional Routine 5. To implement this strategy:

1. Assign each student a different word from the unit.

2. Students fill out the *Roll the Die* template by writing each of the following on separate sides of the cube:

   a. The word

   b. The definition

   c. A visual representation of the word

    d.   An antonym of the word (or, more generally, what the word is not)

    e.   A synonym of the word (or, more generally, what the word is)

    f.   A sentence from the text that uses the word—with the word replaced by a blank

3. Students cut out the template and tape it to form a three-dimensional cube.

4. To use as a *Review and Play* activity with Instructional Routine 5: In small groups or as a whole class, students play an in-class review game with the cubes. The person who rolls the cube acts as moderator for that particular turn. The side of the cube that shows on top is the starting place. Other students in the group respond by giving one or more of the answers found on the other sides.

Differentiation:

- This may be played as a competition between two or more teams. Teams are awarded points for correct answers.

- You can create a generic form of the die. Each side would name the parts of the cube, such as: define the word, describe a visual image of the word, provide an example, name a synonym of the word, give an antonym, and create a sentence with the word.

- As another variation, you could use regular dice. Assign each number to the parts of the generic die.

- For the generic die and regular dice, students need a listing of words. Using *VMCs* (*Vocabulary Manipulative Cards*), students could draw from a stack of words, then roll the die. After three rounds, students would then select another *VMC* from the stack and repeat the process.

Roll the Die Template

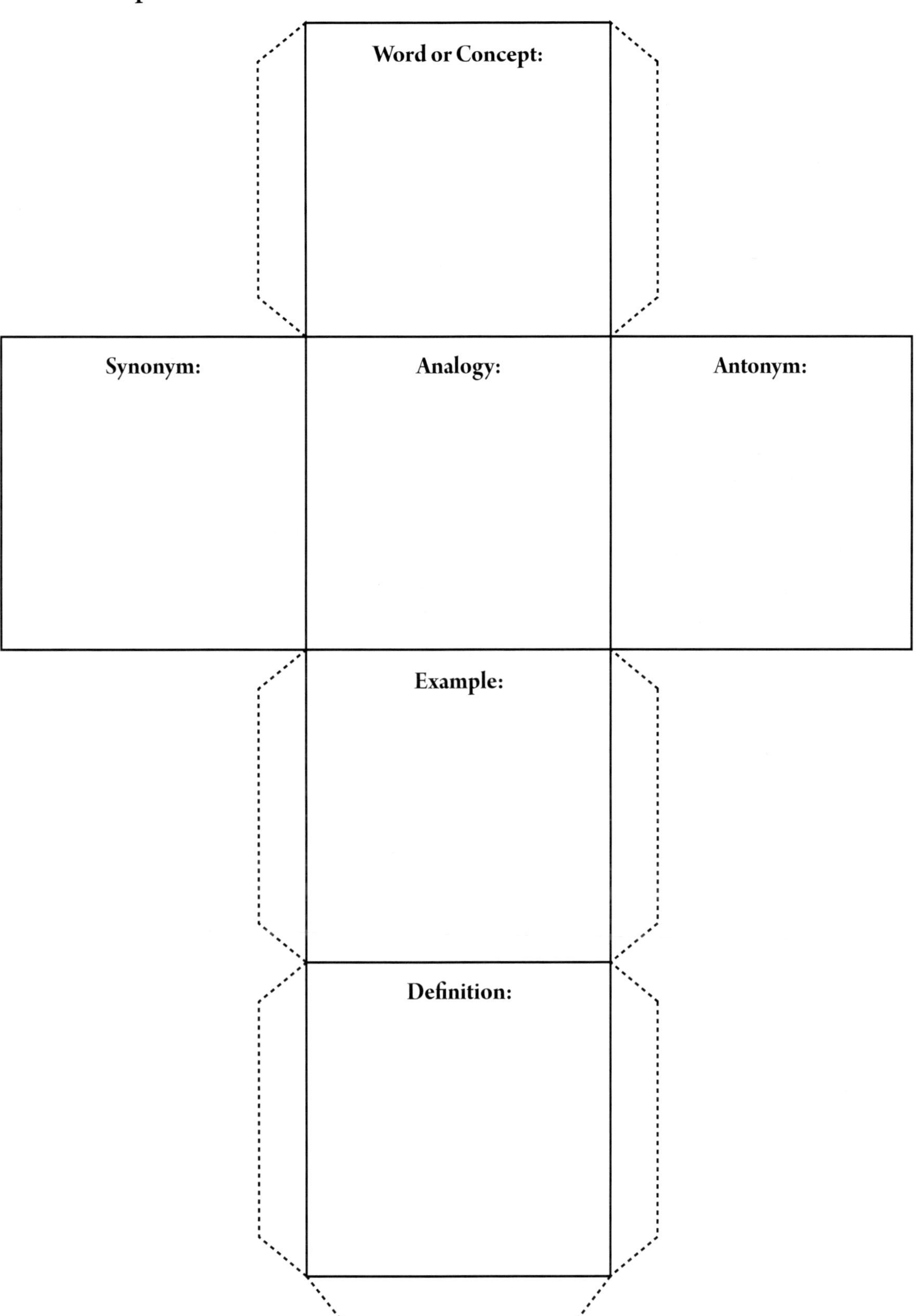

Example: U.S. Constitution Roll the Die

Word or Concept:

United States Constitution

Synonym:
law, national character or complexion, act, enacted customs, ordinance, statute, regulation, canon, Decalogue, establishment, charter, charge, caveat, code, Due Process

Analogy:
living organism

brain and the human body

roots of a tree

Antonym:
breaking, lawlessness, transgression, violation, disorganization, anarchy, deregulation, mismanagement , dictatorship, totalitarianism, immorality, unethical

Example:
Ten Commandments

Pirates' Code

Code of Hammurabi

Definition:
The U.S. Constitution defines the three branches of government, distribution and organization of power, and the rights and responsibilities of citizens.

Example: MLK, Jr. Roll the Die

Roll the Die can also be used to form concepts or to describe events. These are focus words that required details to explain the meaning of the words. These student cubes were created to explain Martin Luther King, Jr.'s views and contributions to the American Civil Rights Movement. After reading and listening to Martin Luther King, Jr.'s "I Have a Dream" speech, students used their die to: associate it, define it, describe it, compare it, connect it (historically), and connect it (personally). The following images illustrate student applications.

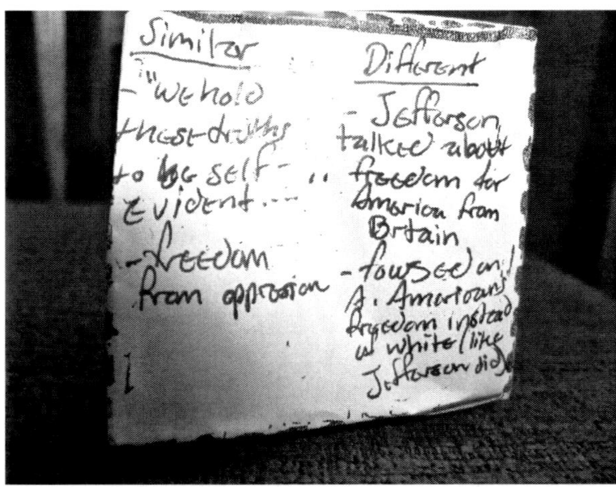

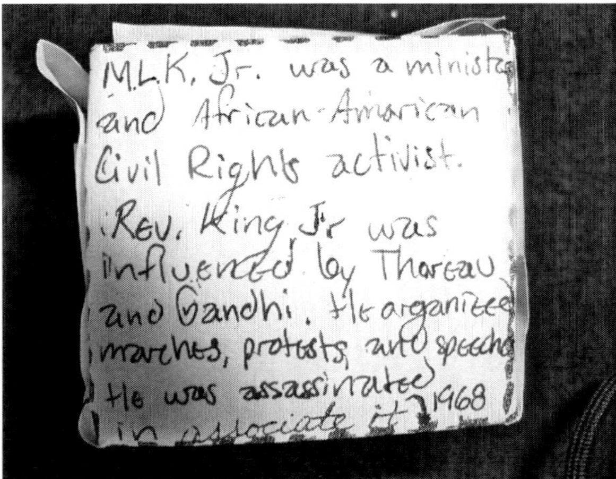

Example: Generic Roll the Die

You can create a generic form of the die. Each side would name the parts of the cube, such as: define the word, describe a visual image of the word, provide an example, name a synonym of the word, give an antonym, and create a sentence with the word. Students would then use a word list and roll that die to play the game. You can include word or concept, as pictured, to require students to verbally state the word to improve their ability to pronounce difficult words. You could also replace "word or concept" with "sentence." Students would then be expected to create a sentence using the word if their die landed on this option.

Generic Roll the Die Template

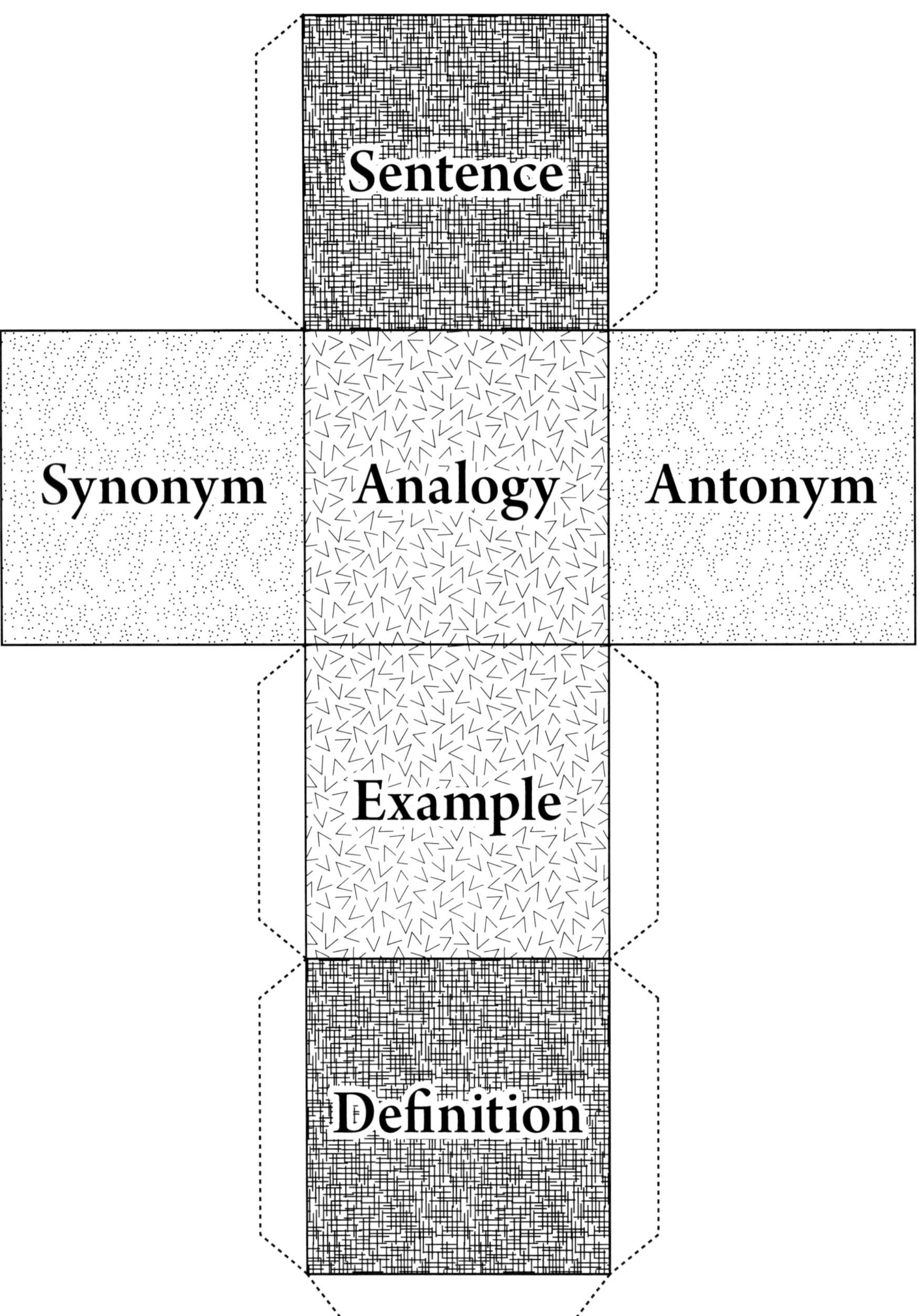

 Permission granted to reproduce for classroom use only. ©2012 Social Studies School Service. (800) 421-4246. www.socialstudies.com

Example: Multiple Regular Dice for Roll the Die

As another variation, you could use regular dice. Assign each number to the parts of the generic die. For example, you could make synonym = 1, antonym = 2, analogy = 3, example = 4, definition = 5, and sentence = 6. If you have multiple die, you could give each member of a group a die. It works best if you have different color dice. If students are grouped in threes, one student would have an orange die, another blue, and the third pink. Students then roll their assigned colored die at the same time. Each student would each take the action that is associated with the number. As an example, the pink die student would name an antonym (die landed on 1), the orange die student would describe an analogy (die landed on 3), and the blue die student would give an example (die landed on 4). Once complete, students would roll their die again and repeat the process. The use of multiple colored die expedite the process of Roll the Die and increase student engagement with word learning strategies.

◎ Application 10: Concept Associations

The *Concept Associations* strategy uses etymologies, synonyms, antonyms, and analogies to teach target word meanings. Raising student awareness of word origin, history, and meaning change over time will increase student reading comprehension and overall understanding of content area text. You can use these types of activities briefly at the beginning or end of a lesson or unit. This process is applicable with words with meanings that have changed over time, but it is also useful with contemporary concepts. The strategy emphasizes word meaning through word parts, synonyms, antonyms, and analogies. With *Concept Associations,* students are answering these questions:

- What are different ways of thinking about the target word?

- What is the original meaning of the word and has this changed over time?

- What do the root words, prefixes, and suffixes explain about the meaning of this target word?

To use *Concept Associations,* follow these steps:

1. Draw attention to words that are no longer used or that have changed meaning over time (see the following examples).

2. List a series of words on the board that have the same root. Ask students to identify what the roots mean, giving a reason for their answer. Additionally, they should list other words that would fit the list. Ask students who finish early to look up the etymology of the word.

3. Have students examine long and unfamiliar words. After dividing the words, they can assign meaning to the individual parts and then guess at the whole word's meaning.

4. Draw attention to suffixes and prefixes, ensuring that students know their meanings and the impact they have on the root word. Use activities that require students to identify and sort words based on their morphology.

Words That Are No Longer or Rarely Used

- kedgebelly—glutton (1811)

- gogmagocical—gigantic (1922)

- culch—lots of rain (1900)

- skingy—cold weather (1855)

- canvas opera—circus (1934)

- shumpgullion—glutton (1896)

- shazzying—dancing (1924)

- cataglottism—lascivious kiss (1893)

- speakeasy—establishment that sells alcohol (1888); also known as blind pig or blind tiger

Words That Have Changed in Meaning

- *Counterfeit* once meant a legitimate copy.

- *Brave* once implied cowardice.

- *Zeal* has become a positive characteristic, but *zealot* still refers to an extremist.

Words Have Stories[7]

- Sabotage: Sabots are wooden shoes. Workers in Holland threw their sabots into machinery during the industrial revolution as a means of protesting working conditions.

- Grim Reaper: The Grim Reaper can be traced to ancient Greeks and Romans who referred to him as Cronus or Saturn, respectively. The Grim Reaper, as often pictured, is associated with the Middle Ages and the Black Death.

---

7 These examples come from *The Mother Tongue* (Bryson, 1990). To discover the history behind words, see http://www.etymonline.com/ and *The Story of English* (McCrum, Cran, & MacNeil, 1986).

Concept Associations Template

Concept Associations	
Concept:	
Root Words:	**Root word and meaning:** Prefix: Suffix:
Originated from:	Originated during: Original use to describe: French word is: Latin word is: Greek word is:
Definition:	
Synonym:	**Antonym:**
Analogy:	

Example: Economics Concept Associations

Concept Associations	
Concept:	Economic Policy
Root Words: Economic Policy	**Economic** *e* = out, away *co* = together, with, join *eco* = live or alive; derives from *oikoc* (ikos) meaning "house, home" *nom* = law or order *my* = muscle Suffix: *ic* = of, relating to, pertaining to, or characterized by **Policy** *poli* = city Suffix: cy = state, condition, or quality
Originated from: Economy	Originated during: 1520–1530 Original use to describe: management of household, property, land French word is: *economie* Latin word is: *oeconomia* Greek word is: *oikonomía* (*oîko*) (*s*) house + -*nomia* -*nomy*
Definition:	Economic policy defines the actions that the government takes to influence the economy for the purpose of managing the nation's human, natural, and capital resources.

Synonym:	Antonym:
• Financial system that manages and controls wealth, marketplace, and nation • Cost-effective and thrifty procedures for managing resources, including money, materials, and labor • Frugal actions of the state or government • Prudent decision making	• Wasteful and lavish • Extravagant and uneconomical • Reckless decision making, without planning and thought

Analogy:

Game plan of an athletic team. Strategy for how to win.

(e.g., be profitable and efficient with the human resources—players)

◎ Application 11: Memory Aids and Mnemonics

Memory Aids are mnemonic devices that you can use to increase student success in remembering important facts, such as lists, places on maps, and key events or people. *Mnemonics* originated from the Greek word *mneme*, meaning "memory," and *mnemon*, meaning "mindful." *Mnemonics* are purposeful strategies for memorizing and assimilating information with existing schema. Using *Mnemonics* will help students master target words. Memory aid activities, which are often fun, are not intended to be repetitious, or rote learning techniques, or used with trivial and obscure information (Joyce, Weil, & Calhoun, 2009). Various uses of *Mnemonics* will help students avoid confusion when they have to remember lots of information or repetitious learning, such as map identification tasks. We also recommend use of *Mnemonics* with students who are less familiar with content or struggle with retaining large amounts of content.

Memory Aids

Letter Strategies

Students use the first letter of each part of a connected series to make an acronym.

In this student example, the student created a letter strategy to remember the 4th Amendment and Due Process.

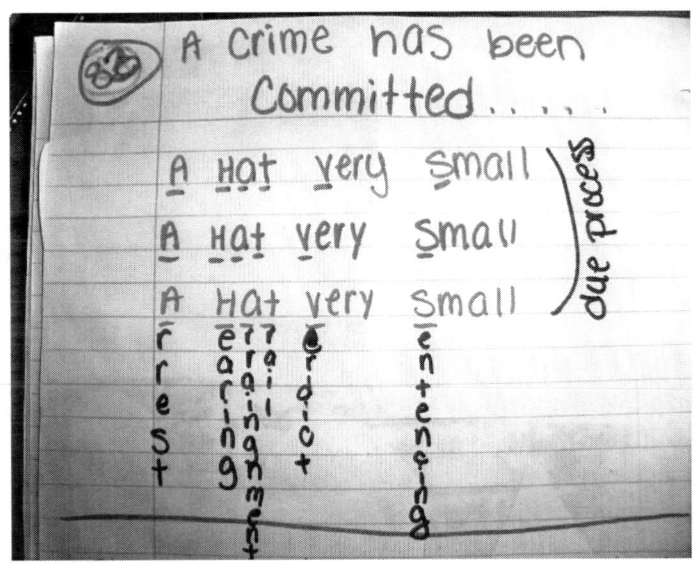

You can also create examples to aid student memory. Examples include:

The 1st Amendment **RAPPS**

- **R**-Religion, **A**-Assembly, **P**-Press, **P**-Petition, **S**-Speech

Order of appointment of current U.S. Supreme Court Justices:

Studying **S**unshine **K**eeps **T**he **G**iant **B**each **R**obots **A**ll **S**andy

- Stevens, Scalia, Kennedy, Thomas, Ginsburg, Breyer, Roberts, Alito, Sotomayor

The four directions:

Never Eat Sour Watermelon

- **N**orth, **E**ast, **S**outh, and **W**est

To recall the names of the Great Lakes:

HOMES

- **H**-Huron, **O**-Ontario, **M**-Michigan, **E**-Erie, **S**-Superior

You can research more social studies-related examples at http://www.mnemonic-device.eu/mnemonics/ or have students create their own.

Chunking

Use this method to break down large amounts of information into smaller, easier-to-remember groups. One way you do this without even knowing it is when you memorize a phone number or your social security number. To remember phone numbers you break the numbers into smaller groups (910-555-1234 or 222-33-1111). Another way to use *Chunking* in school is with vocabulary words. Students can break down words into smaller parts—for example, *together* becomes *to-get-her*. This strategy can be modeled by you and then used by students. When students chunk their own words or information, they are more likely to remember the words. Student examples include: totalitarian becomes total-I-tarian and dict-a-tor-ship is dictatorship.

Picture Associations

These are visualization strategies in which students use images to represent words and word meanings. To use this strategy, have students choose a key word and draw an illustration that will help him or her recall the information at a later date. Students can use clip art or draw their own images. Two student examples of *Picture Associations* for the Bill of Rights follow. In the second example, the student created the *Picture Association* on a *VMC*. The third example presents student-created images of important U.S. Supreme Court Cases from a Civics class.

Example: Amendment 2: Right to Bear Arms

Example: Amendment 19: Women's Suffrage

Example: U. S. Supreme Court Cases

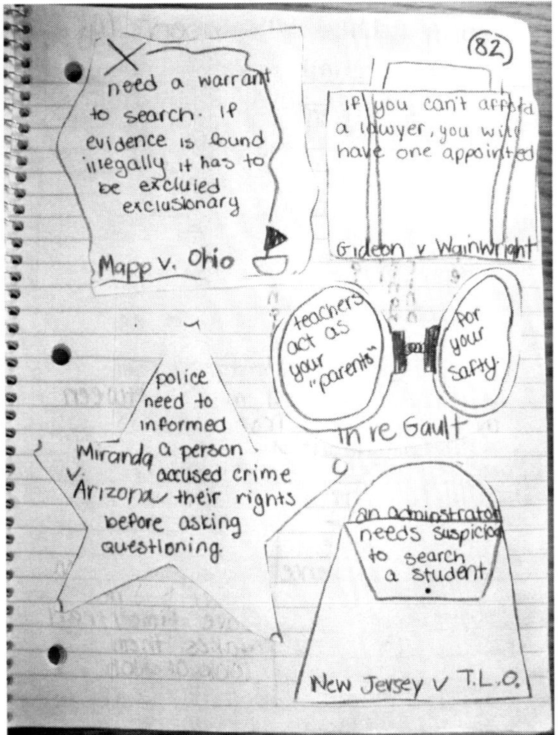

Numeric Memory Aids

This is a great tool for helping students remember sequence or number (i.e., the order of U.S. presidents or constitutional Amendments). Students assign each number a corresponding visual and then use illustrations or rhymes to connect the two. A childhood example is "one, two buckle my shoe…" Another application would be to associate words directly with numbers (1 is run, 2 is shoe, 3 is trees). You can use rhyming words or make picture associations with words. This strategy works well when you have the class work together to create associations for numbers. You might use this technique to help students remember the order of the major Acts passed by the British Parliament leading to the American Revolution—1 is for the Sugar Act (1764), 2 is for the Stamp Act (1765), and 3 is for the Townshend Acts (1767). Picture associations can be used to present visual images of each of these acts. For example, 1 is a sugar bowl, 2 is a stamp, and 3 is a dollar sign.

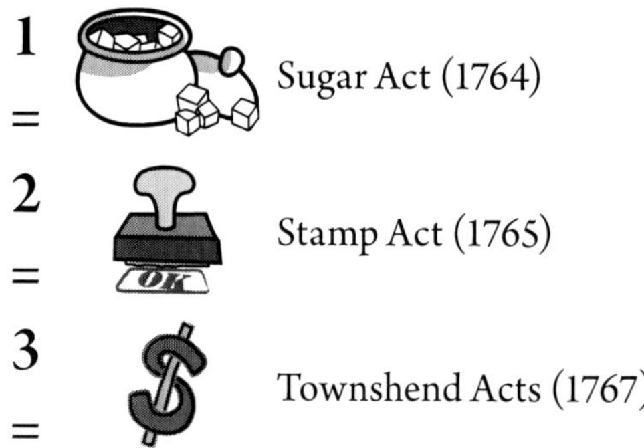

Key Word Strategies

To use this strategy, have students choose a familiar word and associate it orally with an unfamiliar target word. Then ask students to create an illustration or story that further links the two words. Typically these words are similar in sound. For example, you might use *craft* to represent *William Howard Taft* or *comics* for *Economics*. If you struggle with rhyming, there are Web sites that can help you. These Web sites are good sources for finding words that rhyme: http://www.rhymer.com/ and http://www.rhymezone.com/.

Substitute Word Strategies

For this strategy, students take any word or phrase that seems abstract and think of something that sounds like it. For example:

- Alaska = "I'll ask her"

- Darwin = dark wind

- Sweden = sweet den

- Finland = Fins (fin land)

You can then take it a step further and ask students to add a picture to go along with the phrase that uses the new word and reiterates the word to be remembered (Joyce, Weil, & Calhoun, 2009, pp. 203–205).

Link-Word Strategy

The *Link-word Strategy* involves linking an unknown word to a familiar word in order to remember it. This video describes and shows how the method works: http://www.youtube.com/watch?v=9NROegsMqNc. Students will need to use *Link-word Strategy* to capitalize on the benefits of this mnemonic device. Students have to connect unfamiliar words with familiar information in their everyday lives. To use this strategy, you can have students think about the rooms in their home and then associate a different type of economic system in each room. As students move mentally through their home they talk through why they put each word into the specific room. The connection to something well known, such as their home, will help students recall words. The associations they make can also link word meanings.

Rhyming Words Strategy

This strategy involves creating a memorable rhyme to explain a term's meaning. A familiar example is "In 1492, Columbus sailed the ocean blue." You and your students can work together to create rhymes to remember chunks or lists of information as well as connect dates with events or people. The following example illustrates how students might remember the fates of the six wives of Henry VIII; they could use the following rhyme:

> *Divorced, Beheaded, Died,*
> *Divorced, Beheaded, Survived*

A way to remember when the United States expanded to include the states of Alaska and Hawaii:

> *'59 was the date,*
> *When Alaska and Hawaii became new states*

Music and Memory Strategy

Information set to words can help students recall details in sequence or complex ideas. Students can create their own words to familiar tunes like *Yankee Doodle* or *William Tell's Overture* or create their own songs in any musical genre. They can draw from existing resources, such as versions of "The U.S. Presidents' Song," to learn the order of all U.S. presidents (such as the example at http://www.youtube.com/watch?v=oc3xTj3g9QQ).

Instructional Routine 4: Conclusion

Defining and Associating asks students to consider the meaning of words, how these meanings were derived and what associations can be made with words and concepts. This instructional routine presents strategies that unpack word meanings and help students unravel connections among words. These activities guide students to consider multiple words at the same time and provide students with opportunities to gain in-depth knowledge of some words. The number of words you teach with this level of depth is much fewer than you can cover with strategies described in the first three instructional routines. The choices that you make in what words to teach are important; thus, strategies for how to level words to maximize time are present in this chapter. Additional activities provide further variations of complex word learning strategies. These are inductive thinking methods whereby students group information into categories to create symbolic associations. The key to vocabulary learning success as described in this instructional routine is to have students make connections so that learning happens not by repetition but rather by association. These strategies also extend the number of exposures students have with words and offer multiple pathways to learning words.

INSTRUCTIONAL ROUTINE 5: REVIEWING AND PLAYING WITH WORDS

Applications

1. I Have, Who Has?

2. Pictionary®

3. Scattergories®

4. Vocabulary Bingo

5. Who Am I?

6. Who, What, Where Am I?

7. Roll the Die

8. Taboo®

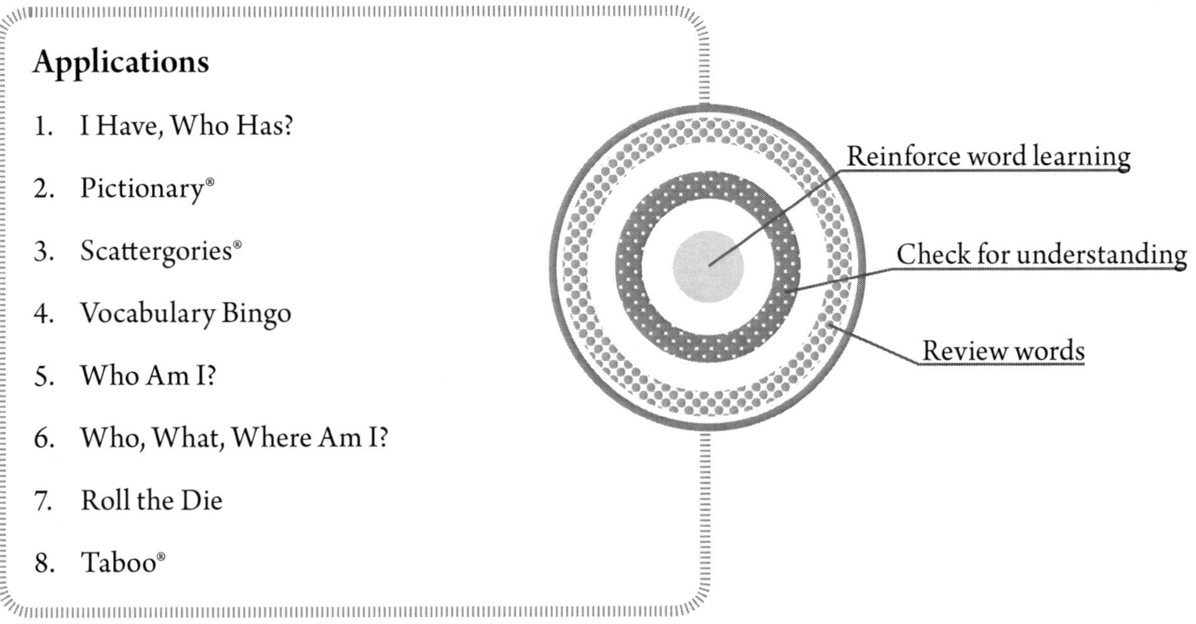

Reviewing Words to check for understanding is essential. Reinforcing word learning is an ongoing process. To gain a complex understanding of a word, students need multiple exposures to the word. Stahl and Nagy's research (2006) suggested that students needed at least twelve interactions with a word in order to solidify the learning. *Playing with Words* offers a motivating way to engage students with the words and provide the multiple exposures needed. *Playing with Words* can also serve as both informal and formative assessments of student learning. Students too can self-assess their word understanding as they participate in word reviews or word play.

Playing with Words becomes a strategy for review and an extension of vocabulary learning. You can offer review games as a whole-class activity or with small groups. Students can also use various technology tools to play with words on their own or with partners.

Questions for *Playing with Words* should help students notice words that still confuse them or that they cannot connect to the overall concept. As students review and play with words, ask these comprehension word focus questions:

1. How confident am I in knowing the word meaning?

2. What words are still confusing? Why?

3. Can I explain how these words connect to the overall concept?

◎ Application 1: I Have, Who Has?

This is a during-reading or post-reading activity for reinforcing and reviewing key vocabulary. To implement this strategy:

1. Prepare a deck of cards based on the number of students in your class.

2. On each card write "I Have" followed by a target word.

3. Then write "Who has?" followed by a brief definition of the next target word.

4. Distribute cards in a random order, giving each student one card.

5. Identify a starter card and have that student read it aloud.

6. The student who has the word that corresponds with the definition read by the first student responds by stating, "I have ______," and then reads the second sentence, "Who has ________?"

    Play continues until the first participant hears the definition for the word on his or her card.

To meet the needs of all students, you can make these modifications to the game:

-   Students needing a challenging enrichment activity can create the cards.

-   If there are more cards than players, you can give students two cards.

Example: I Have, Who Has?

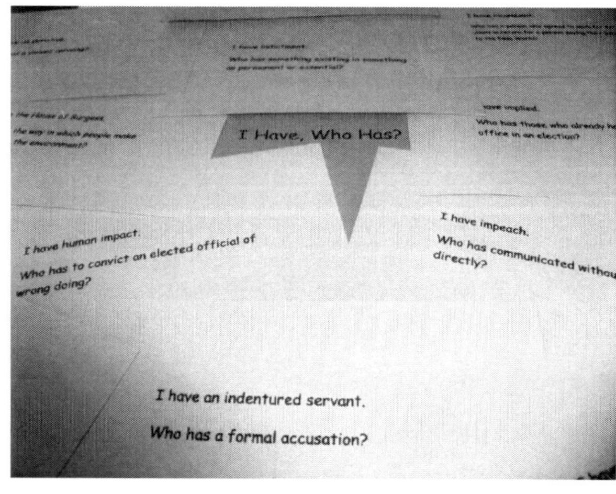

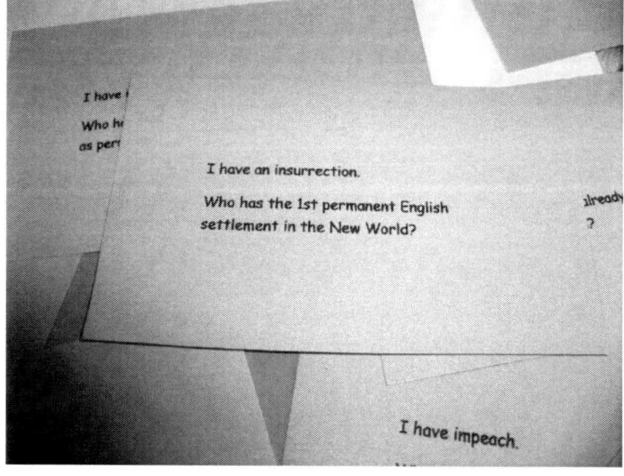

Example: I Have, Who Has…. The American Revolution

I have Thomas Jefferson.   *Who has a colonist against British rule?*[8]
I have a Patriot.   *Who has a meeting of representatives of the British colonies?*
I have the Continental Congress.   *Who has American colonist who spoke out in the Virginia legislature against paying British taxes, and who, when his views became widely known, was accused of treason by Loyalists?*
I have Patrick Henry.   *Who has an event in 1773 when colonists dumped tea from British ships into Boston Harbor?*
I have the Boston Tea Party.   *Who has a soldier in the first colonial army, which was headed by George Washington?*
I have a continental.   *Who has a sudden, complete change of government?*
I have a revolution.   *Who has second U.S. President, champion of independence in 1776, a Federalist, a statesman, lawyer, and diplomat? He was a delegate from Massachusetts to the Continental Congress and assisted in drafting the Declaration of Independence.*
I have John Adams.   *Who has a believer in a peaceful settlement of differences?*
I have a pacifist.   *Who has a location in southeastern Pennsylvania on the Schuylkill River; site of General Washington's winter headquarters during the Revolutionary War?*
I have Valley Forge.   *Who has an agreement signed by British and American representatives on September 3, 1783?*
I have the Treaty of Paris.   *Who has an American who warned the patriots that the British were marching toward Concord, where Patriot weapons were stored?*

---

8 Starter card. Begin by stating, *"Who has a colonist against British rule?"* The student who has, " I have a Patriot," responds.

I have Paul Revere.

Who has to provide or pay for housing?

I have quarter.

Who has to use warships to prevent other ships from entering or leaving a harbor?

I have blockade.

Who has American leader who was sent to Britain to ask Parliament for representation? He was a writer of the Declaration of Independence, a delegate to the Constitutional Convention, and a respected scientist and business leader.

I have Benjamin Franklin.

Who has a synonym for complaint?

I have grievance.

Who has a troop of soldiers?

I have a regiment.

Who has the unanimous Declaration of the thirteen colonies of the United States of America that was signed on July 4th, 1776?

I have the Declaration of Independence.

Who has a synonym for loyalty?

I have allegiance.

Who has a group set up in each of the colonies to quickly share information about taxes and other issues by writing letters to groups in other areas?

I have Committee of Correspondence.

Who has to undo a law or tax?

I have repeal.

Who has freedom to rule one's own?

I have independence.

Who has an American General who defected to the British side?

I have Benedict Arnold.

Who has a speaker at the House of Burgesses who said "Give me liberty or give me death" in 1775?

<table>
<tr><td>

I have Patrick Henry.

Who has a word that means to join?

</td></tr>
<tr><td>

I have enlist.

Who has a person who a member of the Massachusetts colony
militia who could quickly be ready to fight the British?

</td></tr>
<tr><td>

I have a Minuteman.

Who has a Founding Father who was the main writer of the Declaration of Independence, a delegate to the
Constitutional Convention, and the third President of the United States of America?[9]

</td></tr>
</table>

◎ Application 2: Pictionary®

This activity offers a great review of target vocabulary following completion of a thematic unit of study. *VMCs* are great resources for playing *Pictionary®*. To play this game, follow these steps:

1. Create a stack of cards, each containing one relevant vocabulary word.

2. Design effective peer groups. Divide students into teams.

3. Assign each team an order of play—youngest to oldest, reverse alphabetical order, birth month order, the tallest or shortest, and so on.

4. The first student selects a card and comes to the front of the room. He or she "draws the word" based on knowledge of its meaning. Students cannot use written or spoken words.

5. The player's teammates must guess what the word is in less than two minutes. If time runs out, the other team is given the opportunity to guess.

To meet the needs of all students, you can make these modifications to the game:

- Both teams can play simultaneously. The team who guesses correctly first receives the point.

- Reverse the game for a bigger challenge. The player who is "it" must draw based on clues given by his or her teammates. The player has only two minutes to figure out which word is indicated by the clues given.

Example: Civil Rights Movement Pictionary®

In small groups of three or four, work together to review the key people, Amendments, legislation, and social actions of the civil rights movement. Treat this as a competition among groups. Each group has one representative who selects a card (see samples below). Then draw symbols or examples of the following

---

9 The starter card ends the activity by responding "I have Thomas Jefferson" when the final *Who Has* question, *"Who has a Founding Father who was the main writer of the Declaration of Independence, a delegate to the Constitutional Convention, and the third President of the United States of America,"* is posed.

vocabulary. Group members attempt to identify the key terms in the time allotted for the task. Allow one to two minutes for each vocabulary card.

Civil Rights Movement Pictionary Your word to draw is… Thirteenth Amendment	*Civil Rights Movement Pictionary* Your word to draw is… Fourteenth Amendment	*Civil Rights Movement Pictionary* Your word to draw is… Fifteenth Amendment	*Civil Rights Movement Pictionary* Your word to draw is… Twenty-fourth Amendment
Civil Rights Movement Pictionary Your word to draw is… Racial Equality	*Civil Rights Movement Pictionary* Your word to draw is… Passive Resistance	*Civil Rights Movement Pictionary* Your word to draw is… Civil Disobedience	*Civil Rights Movement Pictionary* Your word to draw is… Segregation
Civil Rights Movement Pictionary Your word to draw is… Montgomery Bus Boycott	*Civil Rights Movement Pictionary* Your word to draw is… Freedom Riders	*Civil Rights Movement Pictionary* Your word to draw is… Black Power Movement	*Civil Rights Movement Pictionary* Your word to draw is… Boycott
Civil Rights Movement Pictionary Your legislation to draw is… Economic Opportunity Act 1964	*Civil Rights Movement Pictionary* Your legislation to draw is… Voting Rights Act of 1965	*Civil Rights Movement Pictionary* Your legislation to draw is… Fair Housing Act of 1968	*Civil Rights Movement Pictionary* Your legislation to draw is… Black Power Movement
Civil Rights Movement Pictionary Your person to draw is… Dr. Martin Luther King Jr.	*Civil Rights Movement Pictionary* Your person to draw is… Malcolm X	*Civil Rights Movement Pictionary* Your person to draw is… Rosa Parks	*Civil Rights Movement Pictionary* Your person to draw is… Lyndon Johnson

◎ Application 3: Scattergories®

Scattergories® provides an engaging way to review words and link similar concepts. This fun game can be played as a review to reinforce critical vocabulary and promote teamwork. To play this game:

1. Place students in groups of three or four.

2. Declare one of the three categories (i.e., Civil War terms, words associated with economic development, cultural hearths, cultural diffusion, culture).

3. If using the die from the Scattergories game, have a student roll the die to select a letter of the alphabet. If there is no die, ask a student to choose a letter of the alphabet.

4. Have the groups identify as many words as they can that begin with the chosen letter. From the example, students might identify cultural hearth, cultural diffusion, or culture word as associated with the letter C. Locations, additional river names, and other geographical terms can be added.

5. Compare the answers of each group, and award double points for any unique answers.

6. Award double points for any two word phrases that both begin with the target letter.

7. After several rounds, the team with the most points wins.

To meet the needs of all students, you can make these modifications to the game:

- Draw several letters and have students find examples that all relate to the same chosen category.

- Choose several categories and have students find an example for each.

- Have students complete this activity independently if they finish work early or as extra credit on a quiz or test.

◎ Application 4: Vocabulary Bingo

This activity reinforces word meaning through an engaging and friendly competition. Use during or at the end of a unit of study or as a form of test preparation. You can customize BINGO cards you find online (see, for example, http://jc-schools.net/tutorials/vocab/wordo.html) for classroom use. To play this game:

1. Distribute cards and markers.

2. Call out one definition at a time, giving plenty of time for students to locate the correct vocabulary word and cover it with a marker.

3. The first student to complete one full row or column wins.

4. For further review and reinforcement, ask the winning student to identify and define each word.

To meet the needs of all students, you can make these modifications to the game:

- For longer play, have students cover an entire card.

- Allow the student who "wins" first to be the caller of the next game.

◎ Application 5: Who Am I?

This activity will promote collaboration and participation for all students involved. *Who Am I?* forces students to discuss the target vocabulary in a fun and engaging way. This game makes a good wrap-up to a lesson or transition activity. In addition, it is a nice review activity at the end of a chapter or unit.

To play this game:

1. Write the names of people from the unit vocabulary list on sticky name tags. Prepare as many cards as you have students (28 students = 14 words and 14 definitions).

2. Put the sticky name tags on students' backs so that no student can see what name is on his or her back. You can make name tags with lanyards and laminate the cards for reuse.

3. Explain that when you say "go," each student must circulate around the room asking questions of other students to find out what name is on his or her back. Students will use the advanced organizer to document findings as facts to support their inferences in determining *Who Am I?*

4. Challenge students to complete the activity in a given amount of time. Then reshuffle and see if they can work faster the second time.

5. Ask all students to state who they are and all documented information. This process provides another layer of review of targeted vocabulary as students articulate word meanings and significance.

To meet the needs of all students, you can make these modifications to the game:

- Give students place names or vocabulary words instead of people's names.

- For ELLs with limited language skills, record the responses in complete sentences on the board while students play. Have each ELL student "present" his or her word at the end of the game, using your sentences as a scaffold.

Example: Who Am I?

Question	Answer	Classmate Who Helped Me
When did I live?		
Where am I from?		
What did I do?		
Why am I remembered in history?		
What is an interesting fact about me?		

Using Facts to Make Interpretations:

Who am I? ____

"I Am" Variation

1. Select one student to be "I am."

2. The student draws a card and takes a seat on a stool at the front of the room.

3. Students ask the "I am" questions as if they are a person who lives or lived during the time of the current unit. Prohibit "yes" and "no" questions to force more dialogue and raise the level of questioning between the students.

4. The "I am" student answers with "I" statements, as if he or she were the person selected.

5. The student who guesses the correct answer is the next "I am," if time permits.

20 Questions Variation

1. Select one student to be "I."

2. The student draws a card containing one target word from the current unit of study.

3. The students in the classroom ask "yes" or "no" questions, attempting to determine which word the student has selected.

4. Students are allowed up to 20 questions. If it appears that the students will not guess within that number, you can give clues.

5. The student who guesses the correct answer is the next "I," if time permits.

6. For ELLs with limited language skills, record the responses in complete sentences on the board while students play. Have the ELL student "present" his or her word at the end of the game, using your sentences as a scaffold.

◎ Application 6: Who, What, Where Am I?

This is a pre-reading, during-reading, or post-reading activity that you can use to reinforce and review key vocabulary. This activity will promote collaboration and participation for all students involved and force students to discuss the vocabulary. In addition, it makes a nice review activity at the end of a chapter or unit.

1. Prepare laminated cards with vocabulary words based on the number of students in each class. *VMCs* are good resources to use with this strategy.

2. Each card lists the word and ends with a question: Who am I?, What am I? or Where am I?

3. Cards can include definitions, illustrations, examples, synonyms, antonyms, and analogies. You can also include facts detailing information about the word. Note time period information. (See the What Am I? example below.)

4. Distribute cards randomly, taping one card to each student's back.

5. The students' task is to identify the word, define the word, and learn as much as possible about the word. Students move around the class posing questions to their peers, including what are the attributes/characteristics of the form of government I represent? What are examples of this form of government? What is the opposite of this form of government? What is an analogy? Students are required to generate information about the word throughout the process. To conclude the activity, students present their forms of government in a whole-class review as

they describe not only the word but the attributes (what it is and what it is not) and examples of this form of government.

6. Once all students know who, what, or where they are, reconvene the class for a review of the words. Each student presents who, what, or where he or she is and the corresponding definition of his or her word. If where is the object of this task, then require each student to do a map demonstration.

Example: What Am I?

What form of government am I?

Use this strategy at any point in a unit of study. Examples of government cards follow. The three forms of government presented are: direct democracy, Constitutional monarchy, and dictatorship.

A government wherein all citizens can directly participate in the decision-making process. This form of government exercises rule by the people through referendum. The legislative process of lawmaking, veto, and representation engage all citizens. A modern form of this government is Switzerland. **What form of government am I?**	A government ruled by a legislative body and a figurehead based on birthright for ceremonial and traditional purposes. Power of lawmaking resides in the members of Parliament. Great Britain is a contemporary example of this form of government. **What form of government am I?**	A government ruled by one leader who gained power through other means than birthright. Often the single leader uses force for control to maintain absolute power. A historical example of a country with this form of government would be the USSR during the Cold War under the rule of Joseph Stalin. **What form of government am I?**

To meet the needs of all students, you can make these modifications to the game:

- Provide all but the word on the card and have the student figure out the word.

- Distribute words and definitions separately. Tell students they have to find their partners.

- Assign each student a form of government by taping the word to each student's back. Students are not aware of the form of government each is assigned. Instead they circulate the room asking peers the following questions: What are the attributes/characteristics of the form of government I represent? What are examples of this form of government? What is the opposite of this form of government? What is an analogy? Students are required to generate information about the word throughout the process. To conclude the activity, students present their forms of government in a whole-class review as they describe not only the word but the attributes (what it is and what it is not) and examples of this form of government.

◎ Application 7: Vocabulary Jigsaw

The *Vocabulary Jigsaw* technique is a way to help students develop the meaning of words in collaborative groups. Students are assigned to two groups: an Expert group and a Home group.

To implement *Vocabulary Jigsaw*, follow these steps:

1. Divide the class into Expert groups with approximately five students in each group. This is accomplished by giving every student a number from 1–5.

2. Assign each Expert group one word or concept. Each Expert group should have a word that is different from the other Expert groups.

3. In Expert groups, students collaboratively discuss the meaning of their assigned word. They may use the text and other resources if necessary. Their task is to combine their knowledge to produce an accurate and concise conception of what the word or concept means and how it applies to the current unit of study, which they record on the Definition Template.

4. Once Expert groups have completed the definition on one word or concept, students are reorganized into Home groups. Home groups will contain one student from each of the different Expert groups. This is accomplished by giving each student a letter—A, B, C, D, or E. Thus, Expert Group 1 students would be assigned A, B, C, D, or E. Expert Group 2 students would be assigned A, B, C, D, E etc. Students are then asked to reorganize by letters, with all of the As together, all of the Bs together, as illustrated in the organizational charts below. Once in Home groups (assigned letter A through E), students share their word learning from their Expert group, recording these definitions on the Definition Template. At the end of the Home group discussion, every student should have the definition to all of the words that were discussed in the Expert groups.

The following charts show group organization for the Expert groups and the Home groups:

Expert Group Meetings:

Word or Concept 1 Expert Group	Word or Concept 2 Expert Group	Word or Concept 3 Expert Group	Word or Concept 4 Expert Group	Word or Concept 5 Expert Group
Student—Home group A	Student—Home group A	Student—Home group A	Student—Home group A	Student—Home group A
Student—Home group B	Student—Home group B	Student—Home group B	Student—Home group B	Student—Home group B
Student—Home group C	Student—Home group C	Student—Home group C	Student—Home group C	Student—Home group C
Student—Home group D	Student—Home group D	Student—Home group D	Student—Home group D	Student—Home group D
Student—Home group E	Student—Home group E	Student—Home group E	Student—Home group E	Student—Home group E

Home Group Meetings:

Home Group A	Home Group B	Home Group C	Home Group D	Home Group E
Student— Expert Word or Concept 1	Student— Expert Word or Concept 1	Student— Expert Word or Concept 1	Student— Expert Word or Concept 1	Student— Expert Word or Concept 1
Student— Expert Word or Concept 2	Student— Expert Word or Concept 2	Student— Expert Word or Concept 2	Student— Expert Word or Concept 2	Student— Expert Word or Concept 2
Student— Expert Word or Concept 3	Student— Expert Word or Concept 3	Student— Expert Word or Concept 3	Student— Expert Word or Concept 3	Student— Expert Word or Concept 3
Student— Expert Word or Concept 4	Student— Expert Word or Concept 4	Student— Expert Word or Concept 4	Student— Expert Word or Concept 4	Student— Expert Word or Concept 4
Student— Expert Word or Concept 5	Student— Expert Word or Concept 5	Student— Expert Word or Concept 5	Student— Expert Word or Concept 5	Student— Expert Word or Concept 5

Definition Template

Expert Group 1 Word or Concept	Expert Group 2 Word or Concept	Expert Group 3 Word or Concept	Expert Group 4 Word or Concept	Expert Group 5 Word or Concept

Variation

- Ask Expert groups to create analogies, develop synonyms or antonyms, or create a mnemonic device.

- Groups can also illustrate word or concept meanings.

To meet the needs of all students, you can make these modifications to the game:

- Have ELLs work with native speakers or more English-proficient peers. If their language skills permit, consider electing them as the "Expert" to support their self-image and provide oral language practice.

- Add a column to the template where the "Expert" must collaborate with each group to determine the relationship between his or her term and the term assigned to the current group.

- After students become familiar with target words, students share their word learning from their Expert group in a home group where each student articulates his or her understanding of the word meaning. Home groups also can expand their knowledge of different words or concepts through associations with target words.

- Word learning could be derived from a text that is divided into segments where each group is assigned a different portion of text. In this modification, students jigsaw a text reading. Assigned target words would align with the text. Student Expert groups expand their understanding by discussing the word meaning as presented in the text. You can ask students to identify words that are right there in the text and to make connections with other words or generate other examples.

◎ Application 8: Taboo®

Taboo® is a game that can be played as a review of key vocabulary at the end of a chapter or unit. To play this game:

1. Create cards. Place a target vocabulary word across the top of each card. Below each word write a list of five associated words or words likely to be used in describing the target word. To modify the game, you could have students create their own cards.

2. Divide students into two teams and determine an order of play for each team.

3. The first player draws a card and attempts to get his or her teammates to say the word; however, the player cannot use the target word or any of the other five words on the card. Hand gestures are "illegal."

4. If the player's team guesses the word, they receive a point. If they are unable to guess the word, the opposing team gets an opportunity to guess and receive the point.

5. A volunteer from the opposing team stands behind the player to ensure that he or she does not use any of the forbidden words.

◎ Instructional Routine 5: Conclusion

Reviewing and Playing with Words provides you and students with a formative assessment of word learning. Students can check their understanding of words as they play games and review word meanings. This instructional routine provides additional opportunities for word exposures that are fun, engaging and motivating. You can use strategies to informally evaluate student word knowledge. Students too can self-assess their word understanding as they participate in word reviews or word play. *Playing with Words* is a strategy for review and an extension of vocabulary learning. You can offer review games as a whole-class activity or with small groups. Students can also use various technology tools to play with words on their own or with partners. Outcomes of this instructional routine are that students can determine their level of confidence in knowing word meanings, can identify words that are still confusing, and are able to explain interconnections among words and with concepts.

SAMPLE UNIT: WORLD RELIGIONS

The following sample unit shows how all five instructional applications might be used in a single two- to three-week unit. We begin with *Grouping and Mapping* activities to build background knowledge and schema for the unit of World Religions. These activities serve as pre-reading scaffolds to help students read the texts on their own. Next, we help students deepen their understanding of the words by *Comparing & Contrasting* and *Defining* specific words. Finally, we help students review words and encourage self-monitoring of their own understanding through *Playing with Words*. You can spread the following activities over multiple days, allowing students to work with the words regularly. Work can be completed in class as well as outside of class.

◎ Instructional Routine 1: Grouping and Organizing

In this example, students associate words with a particular religion.

Word List: Siddhartha Gautama, enlightenment, Four Noble Truths, Nirvana, suffering, Middle Way, Eightfold Path, compassion, rejection of gods, Three Baskets of Wisdom, Brahma, Vedas, Upanishads, Vishnu, Shiva, soul, atman, reincarnation, India, caste system, Karma, Qur'an, Muslims, svargam, Arabia, Mohammed, Mecca, Five Pillars, paradise, submission, Allah, pilgrimage, mosque, caliph, Moses, Torah, Ten Commandments, Abraham, Torah, Yahweh, Palestine, temple, Rome, Palestine, Jews, Jesus, Yahweh, messiah, "Love the Lord with all your heart," "Love your neighbor," Ten Commandments, Bible, persecution, heaven, hell

Step 1: Grouping. Provide the students with the word list. Ask students to group words into meaningful word families using *Categories and Labels.*

> **Buddhism:** Siddhartha Gautama, enlightenment, Four Noble Truths, Nirvana, suffering, Middle Way, Eightfold Path, compassion, rejection of gods, Three Baskets of Wisdom
>
> **Hinduism:** Brahma, Vedas, Upanishads, Vishnu, Shiva, soul, atman, reincarnation, India, caste system, Karma, svargam
>
> **Islam:** Qur'an, Muslims, Arabia, Mohammed, Mecca, Five Pillars, submission, Allah, pilgrimage, mosque, caliph, paradise
>
> **Judaism:** Moses, Torah, Ten Commandments, Abraham, Torah, Yahweh, Palestine, temple
>
> **Christianity:** Rome, Palestine, Jews, Jesus, Yahweh, messiah, "Love the Lord with all your heart," "Love your neighbor," Ten Commandments, Bible, persecution, heaven, hell

Step 2: Organizing. Next, students organize words in association with a selected passage by using *Predict the Pattern.*

Predict the Pattern

Title of Reading Selection: ____

Directions: Sort the words into probable sections. Once you have sorted the words, write the "gist" statement and the "to discover" statements.

List of words: Siddhartha Gautama, enlightenment, Four Noble Truths, Nirvana, suffering, Middle Way, Eightfold Path, compassion, rejection of gods, Three Baskets of Wisdom, Brahma, Vedas, Upanishads, Vishnu, Shiva, soul, atman, svargam, reincarnation, India, caste system, Karma, Qur'an, Muslims, Arabia, Mohammed, Mecca, Five Pillars, paradise, submission, Allah, pilgrimage, mosque, caliph, Moses, Torah, Ten Commandments, Abraham, Torah, Yahweh, Palestine, temple, Rome, Palestine, Jews, Jesus, Yahweh, messiah, "Love the Lord with all your heart," "Love your neighbor," Ten Commandments, Bible, persecution, heaven, hell

People	Places	Miscellaneous (Use only when you don't know what the words mean.)
Texts	**Beliefs**	**Gist statement…**

Things to discover *(Fill in at least two things you want to discover based on what you need to know to clarify the placement of words and the gist statement)*

1. ____

2. ____

◎ Instructional Routine 2: Mapping and Visualizing

Step 1: Mapping. After students have completed an initial grouping activity, it is useful to visually map the words associated with this unit through a *Word Wall* map. The following map provides an overview of grouped words, as well as a geographic location for the origins of the religion.

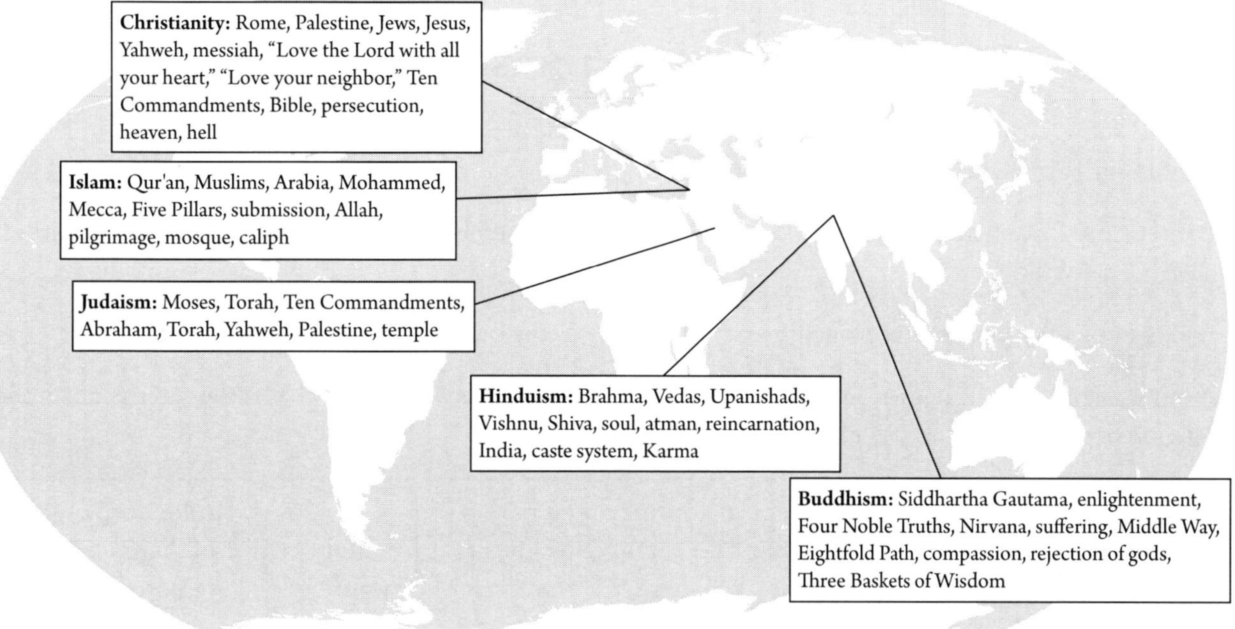

Step 2: Visualizing. Next, students continue to explore words in relation to other words and the visual images that make words memorable. They narrow their focus to one or two words through *Glogs*.

Glogs

1. Choose words from the concept list that can be illustrated.

2. Brainstorm visual representations of the words as a whole class.

3. Assign each student to a group of no more than four students. Each group will be given a single word and a planning sheet.

4. Create a *Glog* at http://www.glogster.com/. The *Glog* should include the word, a visual representation of the word, a paragraph that explains the visual, and the excerpt of text where the word is used.

    There is an example of a *Glog* for world religions—Christianity along with Islam—at http://savannaatk.edu.glogster.com/savannas-religion-glog/

◎ Instructional Routine 3: Comparing and Contrasting

Step 1: Comparing and Contrasting. *Relational Analysis* allows students to examine individual tenets of each of the major religions while comparing and contrasting the religions. The Relational Analysis Chart serves as a scaffold and is especially useful if students are using multiple texts.

World Religions Relational Analysis

The semantic feature analysis will allow contrast of the major tenets between the religions while reinforcing the beliefs of each individual religion.

Directions: Place a mark in the intersection between each member of the word family and the features that have been identified.

A plus sign (+) indicates a relationship exists. Place a + in the box if the religion holds to that belief.

A minus sign (–) indicates the feature does not apply or there is no relationship. Place a – in the box if the religion does not hold that belief.

World Religions	One god	Multiple gods	Suffering is part of earthly life; eternal reward is waiting for those who live right.	Holy writings	Influenced politics of the geographic region during the initial phases.
Buddhism					
Hinduism					
Judaism					
Christianity					
Islam					

Step 2: Compare and Contrast two or more of the religions through the use of a *Venn Diagram*. Small groups of students can use the traditional Venn Diagram to compare two religions, or an expanded Venn Diagram can be used to compare more than two religions.

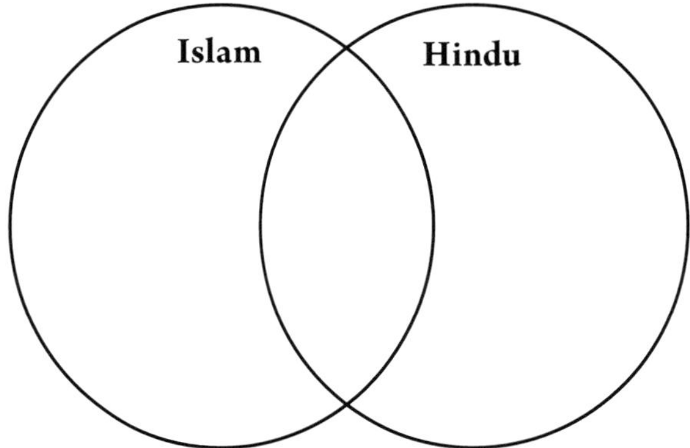

◎ Instructional Routine 4: Defining and Associating

Step 1: Defining. Introduce *Word of the Day* to help students focus on important words. The *Word of the Day* can be displayed on a bulletin board devoted to the unit so that students have an ongoing record of words that have been introduced. Words used for the *Word of the Day* should be different from words you will ask students to define in the next activity, *Squared Up*. The *Word of the Day* may also include etymologies of words, which are available at http://www.worldwidewords.org/index.htm

Select five or ten key words from the word list for defining in the *Squared Up* activity. Our suggested list includes *religion, paradise, messiah, suffering,* and *submission.* These words have multiple meanings, making them ideal for deeper exploration.

Step 2: Defining and Associating. Use *Squared Up* as an individual activity to help students identify specific definitions and make associations to synonyms, antonyms, and other forms of the words. This helps students develop a more nuanced understanding of a word.

Front of card:

Definition: a set of beliefs concerning the cause, nature, and purpose of the universe, especially when considered as the creation of a superhuman agency or agencies, usually involving devotional and ritual observances, and often containing a moral code governing the conduct of human affairs.	**Word:** religion **Other forms of the word:** religious, religiosity	**Synonyms:** devotion, doctrine, orthodoxy, fundamentalism, spiritual **Antonyms:** agnosticism, atheism
Sentence from the text:		**Other words associated with the word:** church, pope, bishop, priest, nun, Vatican, missionary, Roman Catholic Church, rosary, crucifix

Back of card

Illustration/Picture:

◎ Instructional Routine 5: Reviewing and Playing

Step 1: Reviewing the Unit Words. Have students play *Taboo®* to give them repeated exposure to the words. Additionally, use Review and Play to informally assess students' understanding, identifying words and concepts that may still need additional focus.

Taboo®

1. Have students create their own cards to play *Taboo®* as a review of the unit. Have them place a target vocabulary word across the top of each card. Below each word write a list of five associated words or words likely to be used in describing the target word. In the sample shown, "heaven" is the target word while "afterlife," "nirvana," "enlightenment," "paradise," and "reward" are the five words associated with heaven.

2. Divide the students into two teams and determine an order of play for each team.

3. The first player draws a card and attempts to get his teammates to say the word, however, the player cannot use the target word or any of the five words below it. Hand gestures are "illegal."

4. If the player's team guesses the word, they receive a point. If they are unable to guess the word, the opposing team gets an opportunity to guess and receive the point.

5. A volunteer from the opposing team stands behind the player to ensure that they do not use any of the forbidden words during their turn.

Heaven

Afterlife

Nirvana

Enlightenment

Paradise

Reward

◎ Concluding Thoughts

Targeted Vocabulary Instruction

The *Targeted Vocabulary Approach* emphasizes teaching vocabulary as the teaching of concepts, not just words. The five instructional routines for teaching vocabulary in social studies: *Grouping and Organizing, Mapping and Visualizing, Comparing and Contrasting, Defining and Associating,* and *Reviewing and Playing with Words,* are designed to structure student academic vocabulary learning.

5 Instructional Routines: More Than Words

Concept-based, Contextually Driven, Social Studies Vocabulary Instruction

- Reviewing and Playing
- Defining and Associating
- Comparing and Contrasting
- Mapping and Visualizing
- Grouping and Organizing

The five instructional routines move vocabulary instruction along a learning continuum in which early interventions build word awareness while later interventions promote deeper word understanding. The instructional routines encourage learning words through associations to existing schema using a tiered, multifaceted approach. As you use the *Targeted Vocabulary Approach*, you will guide students through organizational strategies that link words into categories, reinforcing particular patterns of thinking such as creating connections and images, and support self-evaluations of learning. These routines reinforce comprehension strategies for reading as students learn words through text-based interventions. Further, the instructional routines help streamline your planning process by creating a logical sequence of vocabulary instruction. Additionally, the activities suggested in the routines offer specific options for differentiating learning in order to meet diverse student needs. Finally, the *Targeted Vocabulary Approach* offers a logical framework for providing students with the multiple exposures to vocabulary that are needed for deeper word learning.

The five instructional routines suggest different ways of thinking about social studies words, while the variety of specific activities within each routine offer choice and variation for you and your students. These are targeted strategies for the purpose of improving student vocabulary learning and academic content comprehension. As you integrate the *Targeted Vocabulary Approach* into your practice, remember the important principle that teaching vocabulary is not an isolated process but is an integrated approach to be used frequently throughout every instructional unit.

RESOURCES

Allen, J. (1999). *Words, words, words: Teaching vocabulary in grades 4–12*. York, ME: Stenhouse Publishers.

Allen, J. (2007). *Inside words: Tools for teaching academic vocabulary grades 4–12*. Portland, ME: Stenhouse Publishers.

Allen, J., & Landaker, C. (2005). *Reading history: A practical guide to improving literacy*. New York: Oxford.

Anderson, R. C., & Freebody, P. (1981). Vocabulary knowledge. In J. T. Guthrie (Ed.), *Comprehension and teaching: Research reviews* (pp. 77–117). Newark, DE: International Reading Association.

Antunez, B. (2002). *English language learners and the five essential components of reaching comprehension*. Accessed January 9, 2011, from http://www.readingrockets.org/articles/341#vocab.

Bailey, A. L. (Ed.). (2007). *The language demands of school: Putting academic English to the test*. New Haven, CT: Yale University Press.

Baumann, J. F., Kame'enui, E. J., & Ash, G. E. (2003). Research on vocabulary instruction: Voltaire redux. In J. Flood, D. Lapp, J. Squire, & J. Jensen (Eds.) *Handbook of Research on Teaching the English Language Arts*, (pp. 52–85). Mahwah, NJ: Lawrence Erlbaum.

Bear, D., Invernizzi, M., Templeton, S., & Johnston, F. (2008). *Words their way* (4th ed.). Upper Saddle River, NJ: Pearson.

Beck, I. L., & McKeown, M. G. (1991). Conditions of vocabulary acquisition. In R. Barr, M. Kamil, P. Mosentahl, & P. D. Pearson, *Handbook of reading research* (Vol. 2, pp. 789–814). New York: Longman.

Beck, I. L., McKeown, M. G., & Kucan, L. (2002). *Bringing words to life: Robust vocabulary instruction*. New York: Guilford Press.

Beck, I. L., Perfetti, C. A., & McKeown, M. G. (1982). Effects of long-term vocabulary instruction on lexical access and reading comprehension. *Journal of Educational Psychology, 74,* 506–521.

Beers, K. (2003). *When kids can't read*. Portsmouth, NH: Heinemann.

Bromley, K. (2008). Actively engaging middle school students with words. In K. Hinchman & H. Sheridan-Thomas, *Best practices in adolescent literacy instruction* (pp. 99–131). New York: Guilford Press.

Bryson, B. (1990). *The mother tongue: English and how it got that way*. New York: William Morrow.

Common Core State Standards Initiative. (2010). *Common Core State Standards for English Language Arts & Literacy in History/Social Studies, Science and Technical Subjects.* Accessed May 5, 2011, from http://www.corestandards.org/the-standards/english-language-arts-standards.

Conley, M. (2008). Cognitive strategy instruction for adolescents: What we know about the promises, what we don't know about the potential. *Harvard Educational Review, 78,* 94–106.

Cruz, B. C., & Thornton, S. J. (2009). *Teaching social studies to English language learners: Teaching English language learners across the curriculum.* New York: Routledge.

Curriculum standards for social studies: Expectation of excellence. (1994). Washington, DC: National Council for the Social Studies.

Davis, F. B. (1942). Two new measures of reading ability. *Journal of Educational Psychology, 33,* 365–372.

Davis, F. (1994). *Fundamental factors of comprehension in reading. Pyschometrica, 9,* 185–197.

Dixon-Krauss, L. (2001). *Using literature as a context for teaching vocabulary. Journal of Adolescent & Adult Literacy, 45,* 310.

Epstein, T. (2009). *Interpreting national history.* New York: Routledge.

50-state report card. (2009). *Education Week, 28*(17), 7.

Fredericks, A. D. (2001). *Readers theatre for American history.* Englewood, CO: Teachers Idea Press.

Gibbons, P. (2002). *Scaffolding language, scaffolding learning: Teaching second language learners in the mainstream class.* Portsmouth, NH: Heinemann.

Glasgow, N., & Farrell, T. S. (2007). *What successful literacy teachers do: 70 research-based strategies for teachers, reading coaches, and instructional planners.* Thousand Oaks, CA: Corwin Press.

Graves, M. F. (2000). A vocabulary program to complement and bolster a middle-grade comprehension program. In B. M. Taylor, M. F. Graves, & P. van den Broek (Eds.)., *Reading for meaning: Fostering comprehension in the middle grades* (pp. 116–135). Newark, DE: International Reading Association.

Graves, M. F. (2006). *The vocabulary book: Learning and instruction.* New York: Teachers College Press.

Graves, M. F. (Ed.). (2009). *Essential readings on vocabulary instruction.* Newark, DE: International Reading Association.

Greenwood, S. (2002). Making words matter: Vocabulary study in content areas. *Clearing House, 75*(5), 258–263.

Guthrie, J. T. (Ed.). (2008). *Engaging adolescents in reading.* Thousand Oaks, CA: Corwin Press.

Heafner, T. L., & Spooner, M. (2008). Promoting learning in a professional development school: Helping students "get over the mountain." In I. N. Guadarrama, J. M. Ramsey, & J. L. Nath (Eds.), *University and school connections: Research studies in professional development schools (Research in professional school development)* (Vol. 3, pp. 117–150). Charlotte, NC: Information Age Publishing.

Hiebert, E. H. (2011). *Growing capacity with the vocabulary of English language arts programs (Reading Research Report #11.02)*. Santa Cruz, CA: TextProject, Inc.

Hinchman, K., & Sheridan-Thomas, H. (2008). *Best practices in adolescent literacy instruction*. New York: Guilford Press.

Irving, J. (2002). *Reading strategies for the social studies classroom*. Austin, TX: Holt, Rinehart, & Winston.

Joyce, B., Weil, M., & Calhoun, E. (2009). *Models of teaching* (8th ed.). Boston: Allyn & Bacon.

Kamil, M. L., Pearson, P. D., Moje, E. B., & Afflerbach, P. P. (Eds.). (2010). *Handbook of reading research* (Vol. 4). New York: Routledge.

Lehr, F., Osborn, J., & Hiebert, E. H. (2004). *A focus on vocabulary*. Honolulu, HI: Pacific Resources for Education and Learning.

Loewen, J. (2010). *Teaching what really happened: How to avoid the tyranny of textbooks and get students excited about doing history*. New York: Teachers College Press.

Marzano, R. J. (2004). *Building background knowledge for academic achievement: Research on what works in schools*. Alexandria, VA: Association for Supervision and Curriculum Development.

Massey, D. S., & Heafner, T. L. (2004). Reading comprehension strategies for social studies. *Journal of Adolescent and Adult Literacy, 48*(1), 2–17.

McCrum, R., Cran, W., & MacNeil, R. (1986). *The story of English*. New York: Viking Penguin.

McKeown, M. G., Beck, I. L., Omanson, R. C., & Pople, M. T. (1985). Some effects of the nature and frequency of vocabulary instruction on the knowledge and use of words. *Reading Research Quarterly, 20*, 522–535.

Moje, E. B., Stockdill, D., Kim, K., & Kim, H. (2010). The role of text in disciplinary learning. In M. Kamil, P. D. Pearson, E. B. Moje, & P. P. Afflerbach (Eds.), *Handbook of reading research* (Vol. 4, pp. 453–486). New York: Routledge.

Moore, D. W., Readence, J. E., & Rickelman, R. J. (1989). *Prereading activities for content area reading and learning* (2nd ed.). Newark, DE: International Reading Association.

Nagy, W. (2005). Why vocabulary instruction needs to be long-term and comprehensive. In E. H. Hiebert & M. L. Kamil (Eds.), *Teaching and learning vocabulary: Bringing research to practice*, (pp. 27–44). Mahwah, NJ: Lawrence Erlbaum.

Nagy, W. E., & Hiebert, E. H. (2010). Toward a theory of word selection. In M. L. Kamil, P. D. Pearson, E. B. Moje, & P. P. Afflerbach (Eds.), *Handbook of reading research* (Vol. 4, pp. 388–404). New York: Longman.

National Council for the Social Studies. (1994). *Expectations of excellence: Curriculum standards for social studies*. Washington, DC: Author.

National Council for the Social Studies Task Force on Standards for Teaching and Learning in the Social Studies. (2008). *A vision of powerful teaching and learning in the social studies: Building social understanding and civic efficacy*, section II. Washington, DC: National Council for the Social Studies. Accessed December 15, 2011, from http://www.socialstudies.org/positions/powerful.

Ogle, D., Klemp, R., & McBride, B. (2007). *Building literacy in social studies: Strategies for improving comprehension and critical thinking.* Washington, DC: Association for Supervision and Curriculum Development.

Pace, J. (2011). The complex and unequal impact of high stakes accountability on untested social studies. *Theory & Research in Social Education, 39*(1), 32–60.

Parker, W. C. (Ed.). (2010). *Social studies today: Research and practice.* New York: Routledge.

Rasinski, T., & Griffith, L. (2007). *Building fluency through practice and performance: American history.* Huntington Beach, CA: Shell Education.

Resnick, B. (2006). *Social studies market, grades K–12.* Rockaway Park, NY: Education Market Research.

Sargent, J. A., & Olney, R. (2011). A case study of vocabulary instruction for high school students. *A Journal of the International Christian Community for Teacher Education, 1*(2), 1–9.

Shanahan, T., & Shanahan, C. (2008). Teaching disciplinary literacy to adolescents: Rethinking content-area literacy. *Harvard Educational Review, 78,* 40–59.

Stahl, S., & Nagy, W. (2006). *Teaching word meanings.* Mahwah, NJ: Lawrence Erlbaum Associates.

Stanovich, K.E. (1986). Matthew effects in reading: Some consequences of individual differences in the acquisition of literacy. *Reading Research Quarterly, 21,* 360- 407.°

Stanovich, K. (1993). Does reading make you smarter? Literacy and the development of verbal intelligence. In H. Reese (Ed.) *Advances in child development and behavior* (Vol. 24, pp. 133-180). San Diego, CA: Academic Press.

Taba, H. (1967). *Teachers' handbook for elementary social studies.* Reading, MA: Addison-Wesley.

Templeton, S., Johnston, F., Bear, D., & Invernizzi, M. (2006). *Words their way: Word sorts for derivational relations spellers.* Upper Saddle River, NJ: Pearson.

Thornton, S. (2005). *Teaching social studies that matters.* New York: Teachers College Press.

Tompkins, G., & Blanchfield, C. (2004). *Teaching vocabulary: 50 creative strategies,* grades K–12. Upper Saddle River, NJ: Pearson.

Tovani, C. (2004). *Do I really have to teach reading?: Content comprehension, grades 6–12.* Portland, ME: Stenhouse Publishers.

Uberti, H. Z., Scruggs, T. E., Mastropieri, M. A. (2003). Keywords make the difference!: Mnemonic instruction in inclusive classrooms. *Teaching Exceptional Children, 35*(3), 56–61.

U.S. Census Bureau. (2011). *Language use in the United States, 2010.* Washington, DC: Author.

Vacca, R., & Vacca, J. (2005). *Content area reading: Literacy and learning across the curriculum* (5th ed.). Boston, MA: Allyn & Bacon.

VanSledright, B. (1998). On the importance of historical positionality to thinking about and teaching history. *International Journal of Social Education, 12*(2), 1–18.

VanSledright, B. (2004). What does it mean to think historically… and how do you teach it? *Social Education, 68*(3), 230–233.

VanSledright, B. (2011). *The challenge of rethinking history education: On practices, theories, and policy.* New York, NY: Routledge.

Wineburg, S. (2001). *Historical thinking and other unnatural acts.* Philadelphia, PA: Temple University Press.

Yarbrough, B. (2007). Why Johnny can't read his textbook. *Hesperia Star.* Accessed May 1, 2011, from http://www.hesperiastar.com/onset?id=656&template=article.html.

WEB SITES

Animation Tools

- http://comiclife.com
- http://goanimate.com
- http://www.toondoo.com

Antonyms and Synonyms

- http://dictionary.reference.com/browse/antonym
- http://www.synonym.com
- http://www.synonym.com/antonym/
- http://www.synonym.org/synonym/
- http://www.thesaurus.com/

Etymology

- http://www.etymonline.com
- http://www.worldwidewords.org/index.htm
- http://www.wordorigins.org/index.php/big_list/

Flash Cards

- http://www.flashcardexchange.com
- http://www.insidestoryflashcards.com
- http://www.kitzkikz.com/flashcards/
- http://museumbox.e2bn.org
- http://www.quizlet.com/

Mnemonics

- http://www.ldonline.org/article/5912
- http://www.mnemonic-device.eu/mnemonics
- http://www.rhymer.com/
- http://www.rhymezone.com/

Presentation Tools

- http://www.glogster.com/
- http://www.prezi.com/

Vocabulary Organizers and Resources

- https://bubbl.us
- http://jc-schools.net/tutorials/vocab/index.html
- http://www.keithschwarz.com/mathtricks/magic.php
- http://www.prezi.com/
- http://www.vocabtest.com/vocabulary_workshop/
- http://www.wordle.net/

